Tell it together

The Bible Reading Fellowship
15 The Chambers, Vineyard
Abingdon OX14 3FE
brf.org.uk

BRF is a Registered Charity (233280)

ISBN 978 0 85746 499 6
First published 2017
10 9 8 7 6 5 4 3 2 1 0
All rights reserved

Text © Renita Boyle 2017
The author asserts the moral right to be identified as the author of this work

Cover image by Rebecca J Hall

Acknowledgements
Scripture quotations taken from The Holy Bible, New International Version (Anglicised edition)
copyright © 1979, 1984, 2011 by Biblica. Used by permission of Hodder & Stoughton Publishers, a
Hachette UK company. All rights reserved. 'NIV' is a registered trademark of Biblica. UK trademark
number 1448790.

A catalogue record for this book is available from the British Library

Printed and bound by CPI Group (UK) Ltd, Croydon CR0 4YY

Tell it together

50 tell-together Bible stories to share

RENITA BOYLE

For my beloved, Eric. Thank you for sharing the big story of God's love
with me through all of the mini-stories along the way.
May this resource truly be a godsend in your life and ministry.

I would also like to dedicate this book to my childhood church in
Reeve, Wisconsin, where I told my first Bible story over 40 years ago.

Pastor, youth worker, parent, teacher, friend, storyteller—
this is my longing for you:

that your life be storied by God's grace;
that you live the big story of God's love;
that you tell the stories of God's word
with passion, purpose and skill.

Acknowledgements

I would very much like to thank everyone in Wigtown and Kirkcowan
parish churches, who are often among the first to hear my stories and
encourage me in their telling.

contents

NEW TESTAMENT STORIES

NEW TESTAMENT PARABLES

Introduction

Storytelling is a vital skill for everyone in ministry. Our entire lives revolve around the big story of God's love for us, how we respond to it and how we help others to respond to it.

The Bible is a collection of stories gathered from oral and written tradition. It reflects both the inspiration of the Holy Spirit and the personalities of the people who penned the stories in it. Hence, it is both deeply sacred and deeply human. Indeed, the writer of Hebrews declares scripture to be alive and active; sharper and more penetrating than the most incisive of swords; able to divide soul and spirit, joints and marrow, and judge the thoughts and attitudes of the heart (Hebrews 4:12, paraphrased). It is, as Paul says to Timothy, useful 'for teaching, rebuking, correcting and training in righteousness' (2 Timothy 3:16).

Like all great stories, Bible stories inform, inspire, entertain, engage, encourage, warn, challenge, heal, comfort and guide. In the tradition of all great storytelling, each generation must come to an understanding of their faith that is both foundational and fresh.

The Bible reveals Jesus Christ, Emmanuel—God become human whose very names mean 'God is with us' and 'God saves'. Through Jesus, we know God's character and have the perfect example of what it means to be human.

Jesus' own use of stories both to reveal and to illustrate truth was so integral to his life and so prolific in his ministry that it is said he never taught without a story. The account of his life, death and resurrection, his words and his deeds, is there to bring us into relationship with God and bring about transformation in us.

Indeed, relationship and transformation are at the heart of all Bible storytelling. Bible stories connect us to God, ourselves and others and demonstrate the change that is possible when we allow the Holy Spirit—the divine Storyteller—to use them to shape our lives.

A well-told story can pull us in and hold us; it can enhance our experience and expression of worship, witness and learning—and that is why I have created this resource.

How to use this book

Ideally, the aim of oral storytelling is to tell stories, rather than to read (or recite) them. In reality, this can be difficult for those who have little time to prepare or lack the confidence to speak to a group unaided. This resource is a hybrid. It combines stories that have been written for you to read well aloud with all the tools that make a great oral participation story for your group to tell together. You could use it on a 'grab and go' basis with little preparation. However, you will get the most out of it (for yourself and for your group) if you use the 'Prepare well, tell well' guidance it contains.

What is a Tell Together?

Tell Together stories or tales involve everyone in some aspect of their telling. The participation is planned but only briefly practised, just before the telling—if it is practised at all. The Bible retellings in this resource have been written as participation stories and contain everything you need to tell them together.

Some of the stories have a simple action or gesture that everyone is prepped to do on cue, or a refrain that is echoed back or repeated throughout the story. Some have a line of a song to sing, a call for a response, a chant or a noise to make. Some involve role play. Some are written with rhythm, rhyme and repetition, others without. Tell Togethers can be told as narratives, eyewitness accounts or from different perspectives. They can be told in a variety of forms: chain tales, topple tales, silly songs or ballads. Some are reflective or liturgical in tone and others are energetic and fun.

Why Tell Togethers?

Participation stories are great for group gatherings, whether all-age or a single age group. They are, by nature, entirely engaging. They provide the irresistible invitation into discovery that is vital to effective storytelling. Everyone is involved in creating an experience that enhances their own worship, witness and learning. As such, Tell Togethers have the potential to be truly transformational. We become part of the stories we tell, and they become part of us.

Our goal, as Bible storytellers, is to allow the Holy Spirit to use us and the stories we tell to bring life and life-change.

Consider how Tell Togethers engage every aspect of our personality.

- Spiritually, they enhance our experience and expression of worship (our relationship and response to God), witness (our relationship and response to each other) and learning (our relationship and response to ourselves).
- Emotionally, they encourage empathy, develop confidence and demonstrate values.
- Creatively, they engage the imagination, inspire creativity and expression.
- Intellectually, they encourage knowledge, appreciation of language, literacy, history and cultural understanding.
- Physically, they give us ways to expend energy, express our emotions and use our voices; they help us to listen and provide a comforting structure.
- Socially, they teach communication and social skills, and help to connect us with one another.

What involves us engages us; what is repeated is remembered; what is remembered is repeated; and what inspires us transforms us.

Where do I start?

This resource is a good starting point. Fifty stories are written for you to read well aloud, providing everything that makes a great participation story for your group to tell together. Words and actions for everyone to say and do together appear in bold in the scripts. You will also find tips to help you prepare well and tell well, one step at a time.

The following two lists will, at a glance, get you thinking about where to start in the development of your storytelling skills. It will be helpful for you to return to them often as a reminder of your progress as you prepare your stories. Each point is explored more fully in the 'Prepare well' and 'Tell well' sections that follow.

Prepare well

- Develop your self
- Choose a story to tell
- Explore the original story
- Explore the retelling
- Know your calling as a storyteller
- Read and rehearse the text aloud
- Know your tools
- Know your group and setting
- Know your desired outcome
- Know how you will begin
- Know how you will end

Tell well

- Be prayerful
- Be positive
- Be comfortable
- Be careful
- Be calm
- Be confident
- Be approachable

- Be organised
- Be clear
- Be heard
- Be aware
- Be respectful
- Be responsive
- Be yourself
- Be measured
- Be flexible

Prepare well

To tell a story well takes advanced preparation—not only of the story but of your self as a storyteller. The process needs time for reflection, practice and the development of storytelling skills. The following section will get you started.

Develop your self

While it is tempting to skip straight to the 'practical bits' of this resource, it is vital not to do so. To be as effective as you can be, you will need to develop your self as well as your skills. True confidence will exude from your own relationship with God and your own story of transformation. This is such a core value in the life of a Bible storyteller that it deserves an entire resource of its own. For now, however, I urge you at least to begin to prepare your self.

- **Honour the Storyteller:** Discover more of God the Holy Spirit who breathed life into the library of stories that you are seeking to retell. How are you relying on the Holy Spirit to enrich you, empower you, gift you and embolden you?
- **Honour the original story:** Discover what the original story means to you personally. Reflect on scripture and let the story transform you and become part of you, your growth and experience. What is the Holy Spirit trying to communicate to you and through you in this story?

- **Honour the experience:** Discover the difference between delivering an entertaining event and creating a transformational experience. Pray and prepare. Expect God to speak and move and transform. How will you create an environment that the Holy Spirit can easily inhabit?
- **Honour your calling:** Discover your calling as a Bible storyteller. How will you let the story you are seeking to retell enhance your own and other people's experience and expression of worship, witness and learning?

Choose a story to tell

The stories in this collection do not cover every story in the Bible. However, they do offer a wide variety to get you started. Please feel free to adapt or write your own versions if you prefer. You may want to tell a story that will stand alone, be used to enhance a theme or Bible passage, or be combined with other activities as the basis for a club meeting or a creative worship gathering or festival. Remember to choose something that is appropriate for the group you will be working with. This may mean not telling some of these stories where there are young children present or where particular sensitivities might be triggered. It may also mean challenging the notion that adults will not enjoy stories that children like.

Ask yourself these questions when choosing a story to tell:

- Do I like this story myself?
- Will I enjoy telling this story?
- Do I care about this story and feel connected to it?
- Will the group like this story and enjoy being part of it?
- What will they need to know or have experienced to relate to this story?
- Will the story work well in the location where I am planning to tell it?
- Will the story fit the tone of the gathering?
- Will this story enhance the theme or Bible passage we are exploring?
- Will this story enhance the experience and expression of worship, witness and learning?

If you like the story yourself and care about what happens in it, you are more likely to spend time preparing it and will most certainly enjoy telling it. This will help your group to connect with you as the storyteller as well as with the story you tell.

If you can imagine how your group will respond to the participation aspects of the story, you will quickly identify where you may need to adapt it. The same is true if you think about where you will be telling the story.

If you spend some time reflecting on how the story fits into the wider context of your ministry, you will naturally enhance the spiritual exploration and journey of your group.

Explore the original story

Seek to understand something of the original story in its biblical context; note points of transformation in the characters you encounter. Ask the following questions.

- What is this story about? Can you summarise the bare bones?
- What is the story *really* about? Do you understand its meaning?
- What type of story is it (for example, poetry, parable or factual)?
- Who are the characters in the story and how are they involved in the events?
- How do the characters change in the story? For example, how do they struggle, discover, and grow?
- What is the setting of the story? Where does it take place?
- What happens in the story? Can you describe the structure and plot?
- What is the context of the story? What happens before and after the events it describes?
- What did the story mean when it was written, to those who were involved in it or first heard it?
- What is timeless about this story? What truth does it reveal or illustrate today?
- What is the Holy Spirit communicating to you through the story? How will you let it transform you and shape your faith?

Explore the retelling

Seek to understand the story you have chosen from this collection. Again, ask some questions.

- What is/are the universal theme(s)? What is familiar to the experience of those in your group, which will provide a point of connection between them and the story?
- What themes may be personal to individuals in the group? Are there any themes that may be sensitive for some people?
- What is the tone of the story (for example, powerful, entertaining or inspiring)?
- From whose point of view is the story told?
- What emotions emerge from the story? What do you need to feel in the story so that you can express it well and help the people in your group to experience it?
- What motivations are present? Identify the motives behind the characters' actions so that the group can understand them.
- Does the story work as a whole? Adapt as necessary for your own style and setting; expand or leave things out.
- What does it leave you reflecting on or questioning? What does it inspire within you? Allow room in your retelling for this to happen for your group.
- How does the story engage you emotionally from beginning to end?
- How is the story sharable? Imagine what the people in the group will talk about or share with others when they leave your presence.
- How does the story enhance the experience and expression of worship, witness or learning?

Know your calling as a storyteller

If Bible stories play any role in your ministry at all, big or small, you are a storyteller. Think of yourself as a storyteller whenever you tell a Bible story and it will make a significant impact on your delivery.

The stories in this resource may be read aloud well, but they are intended to be 'Tell Togethers' and will require preparation as such.

Read and rehearse the text aloud

You will be telling your story aloud, so it is vital to practise it aloud.

Read aloud, read aloud, read aloud, repeat

- Aim to be so familiar with the story that you are able to gain and maintain as much eye contact as possible and rely on the text as little as possible.
- Know the beginning lines of each paragraph, repetitive phrases and points of participation particularly well or off by heart.
- Play with the phrasing: just because something is written in rhyme, it does not mean it has to be overpowered by the rhyme.
- Note where you may be stumbling on words or phrases and smooth them out with practice.
- Aim to familiarise rather than memorise.

Rehearse as you intend to tell

- Pay attention to the places in the story where you will make eye contact, and how you will use your voice, facial expressions and body language. (See 'Know your tools' below.) This will not only help you tell well, but will also give you confidence and be a natural channel for the productive use of nervous energy.
- Although there are elements of performance in storytelling, remember that storytelling is not a performance.
- Participation stories are collaborative by nature and anything but passive.
- Aim to visualise and improvise rather than dramatise.

Refine your skills with feedback

- Rehearse in front of a mirror, into a dictaphone and/or in front of a friend. This will help you to identify any distracting or disturbing mannerisms that you might have, such as fiddling with your glasses or nose, swaying back and forth, bouncing, pacing or screeching.
- Get constructive feedback from others and refine your skills.

Know your tools

Good storytelling (like all communication) involves more than what you say. It involves you—the whole of you. Indeed, the best visual aid you will ever use in storytelling is your body language—your eye contact, facial expressions and gestures. Understand and use the tools you need to tell well.

Use your voice

- **Animation:** Avoid the drone of monotone. Be expressive and dynamic. Raise and lower your pitch within a comfortable listening range. Ensure that the characters in your story, as well as your narrative style, are dynamic and animated.
- **Articulation:** Speak clearly and fluently, and articulate your words and phrases. Exaggerate them. Ensure that your characters also speak clearly and fluently, particularly if they are given their own voice or an accent.
- **Pauses:** Plan pauses carefully. Make effective use of silence as well as speech.
- **Pace:** Speak slowly enough for listeners to catch what you are saying. Change your pace to match the mood of the character who is speaking or to reflect what is happening in the story. However, always speak slowly enough for listeners to hear what you are saying and to grasp it.
- **Pitch:** Avoid high, whiny or screechy speech. Lower the pitch of your voice to the middle of your speaking range for the comfort of your listeners (and your voice). Vary your pitch to suit the dynamics of the story but avoid whining or screeching at uncomfortable levels.
- **Rhythm, rhyme and repetition:** These 'three Rs' are often used in participation stories. They can help you and your listeners to remember the story; they build tension and animation and encourage participation naturally. Over-exaggerate your delivery of these elements to increase the fun-factor or humour in the story or if you want the story to have a lilting musical feel. Seek to deliver them with a more natural flow and speech pattern if the story is sombre in tone.

- **Sounds:** Practise important sounds and sound effects.
- **Tone:** Convey a sense of place, mood, emotion or personality in the way that you speak.
- **Voices:** Plan and practise character voices and accents. Make sure that they are appropriate and inoffensive. Be mindful that the voices you use create an impression.
- **Volume:** Use a volume that is appropriate to your setting. Make it your aim to be heard by everyone without shouting. This will depend largely on the size of your group. As a rule, speak more quietly and intimately to smaller groups and more loudly for larger groups or across larger spaces. You will, of course, need to change the volume as dictated by the characters and situations in your story. Use a stage whisper (which is still loud enough for everyone to hear but gives the appearance of a whisper) or stage shout (which is loud but not deafening to the group) in your telling.

Use your eyes

Whether telling or listening, nothing is more engaging than eye contact. Maintain as much comfortable eye contact as possible, given the size of the group. Each person should feel as though you are telling the story just for them. Look up and look out!

Use facial expressions

Change your expressions depending on the emotional content of the story. Let people see what is happening in the story on your face. This will help your listeners to know how to respond, too.

Use your body

Gestures should be meaningful and simple, natural and relaxed. Practise them ahead of time and you will do them naturally when you tell. Make sure your whole body is telling the same story. Match your body language and gestures to the tone and message of the story and avoid giving mixed signals. Remember, everyone in the group will need to see what you do. On the whole, you will use large, exaggerated gestures for large groups and smaller, less exaggerated gestures for smaller groups.

Knowing what gestures you will use in your story will also help to prevent distracting mannerisms and give your body something to do with its nervous energy.

Know your group and setting

Discover all that you can about the group you are telling to. Who are they—ages, stages, abilities? What are they expecting from your time together? Why are they gathered: is it a regular meeting or a special event? How can you enhance their spiritual journey?

Single-age groups respond differently from mixed-age groups. For example, a story that may seem too young for a teenage or older age group may be perfectly enjoyed and often relished in an all-age setting or a large group where there is safety in numbers.

Family groups that sit together will respond differently from family groups that are scattered. Indeed, family members who listen together can relate to and influence each other, explaining things that may not be understood.

Aim to tell stories that families would be happy discussing, exploring or explaining together.

Make sure you know and understand the place where you are gathering, including the physical surroundings and what issues may arise from them.

Know your desired outcome

Know why you have chosen the story and what you are hoping it will achieve.

Know how you will begin

Think about how you will introduce your story, and prepare a simple set-up for it. Resist the temptation to tell what you are going to tell before you tell it. If you prepare how you intend to introduce your story beforehand, you will avoid being tongue-tied if nerves kick in.

Know how you will end

You will want to let the story speak for itself where possible. Skip the need to express your own opinion or tell people what to think. Prepare reflective, wondering questions beforehand to help your listeners discover meaning for themselves. Let the story speak and the Holy Spirit apply. Remember, 'stories enhance sermons; sermons do not enhance stories'.

Tell well

You have prepared well in advance and have taken the time to reflect, practise and develop your storytelling skills. Now it is time to tell your story and tell it well—putting all that preparation to work for you. This section explains what you will need to think about shortly before you tell and/or during the telling itself.

Be prayerful

Ask God to honour your preparation, use the story and use you to transform others.

Be positive

Expect a good outcome. The attitude you bring with you into your storytelling will have a huge impact on the delivery and impact of your story. Choose to be optimistic, respectful, calm and flexible. Remember, the group are on your side. They want you to do well. The more positive you are, the more positive they will be.

Be comfortable

Wear something that is appropriate for your story and setting, comfortable and easy to move in.

Be careful

Take good care of your voice. Drink lots of water before you start and keep a bottle of water within reach while telling. It is also a good idea to go to the toilet before you start.

Be calm

Accept your nerves but get rid of the jitters. It is only natural to be a bit anxious. Harness these feelings; control your nervous energy and convert it into the warm enthusiasm you will need to tell your story.

Breathe deeply to get oxygen to your brain and help to relax your body. Clench and release your hands. Stretch your limbs and walk around. Slow your speech.

Arrive early and give yourself plenty of time to settle down, relax into the environment and adapt to the space. The more adjusted you are, the more comfortable you will feel.

Strike a superhero pose. Practise an exaggerated power stance for a few minutes in private before entering the space to tell the story. Stand straight and tall, plant your feet, and keep your chest out, head up, hands on hips and a wide smile. This may look and feel ridiculous, but will help you get rid of jitters and create a sense of confidence and assurance to take with you into your telling.

Imagine yourself delivering the story in a calm and confident manner.

Be confident

If you have prepared well, you have laid a good foundation to tell well.

Hold yourself in a comfortable and confident manner before you begin. Remember that your body language will either support or distract from your story.

Make as much eye contact as possible. This will help your group feel valued, connected and attentive. Any time you look down or away, you will place a barrier between you and those you are telling to.

Rely on your written text as little as possible.

Be approachable

Chat with people beforehand. This will help to put everyone at ease, including you. It will also help everyone to feel good about what is coming next. Say hello and smile when it is time for the story.

Be as close as possible to the group. Be aware of what your body is saying, not only during the telling of your story but before and afterwards. Keep an open stance, with arms relaxed at your sides.

Be organised

If possible, get to your venue early and ensure that the space is set up before you start.

Test the acoustics and lighting. Rehearse your story with the microphone, and understand the seating arrangements. Distractions will diminish the experience. Be aware of them (for example, a noisy road outside) and remove them where possible (for example, flowers placed directly in front of you).

Ensure that you can see the words and that they are not a distraction to the group.

Hold the book (or other material) up at chin level. This will help with eye contact and your ability to speak clearly and be heard. Use a stand or a podium if you can, but stand to the side of it. This will free up your hands and body for gesture and movement and ensure that everyone can see you. Avoid holding the book down, dropping your chin or hiding behind the book or podium.

Be clear

Have everyone's attention before you start. Wait quietly or do something to grab attention. Start smoothly and be natural.

Look at everyone; take in the whole group. Can you see everyone and can everyone see you?

Be clear about how you want people to participate in the story. Practise participation elements briefly before you start.

Be clear about your boundaries as well. How close can they get to you? Set a silence signal to help maintain control if necessary.

Be heard

If there is a microphone, use it, especially if you are telling to larger groups in settings where people are spread out over a big space. There will be those who simply cannot hear you without it. With or without the microphone, aim to be heard by everyone. This does not entail shouting or screeching, but requires good use of volume, pitch and clarity of speech. Project your voice.

Be aware

Read the group. Who perks up and looks willing to participate? Who hangs back or looks uncomfortable? Who seems eager and energetic? Who may find it physically difficult to do actions or hear? If your group is scattered, try to draw it together.

Be respectful

Respect the group. Help them to relax; encourage participation at their level of comfort or not at all. Speak respectfully with them, and resist demeaning or chiding them. Are they comfortable? Is there enough fresh air and wiggle room? Warmly eyeball those who are disruptive.

Be responsive

Respond to the group. Adapt to the needs and energy in the room; add more or less participation; change direction or find alternative physical gestures if need be. Encourage the group to respond to you with their eyes and gestures. Storytelling is a give-and-take experience. Help listeners to learn how to be a good audience. Look for verbal and non-verbal communication.

Be yourself

Tell the story your way, as you have practised it. Be authentic.

Be measured

Speak slowly. Your nerves and familiarity with the story will tend to speed you up. Exercise good pacing. Speak slowly enough that the story may be easily absorbed and can be reflected upon, but not so slowly that you bog it down. Vary your tone.

Use the moment you have created and the empathy generated to gently guide personal application. Give people a way to respond, something to do or remember or say or take away. Look for transformational applications and life-changing moments.

Be flexible

Telling well does not mean telling perfectly. Don't worry about mistakes. Try not to draw attention to them. What is lost in eloquence may be made up for with enthusiasm. If information is needed, slide it in. If not, leave it out. Keep a steady flow.

Remember, no matter how well you have prepared, there are a lot of things you will not be able to predict. If attention is lost during the story, gently help people get back on track. Acknowledge what may be happening in the room with a glance or a nod, but don't focus on it.

Prepare well to tell well, and it will also help you to be flexible, come what may.

Old Testament Stories

I

Name this day
The story of creation

For your reflection: Genesis 1:1—2:3; Genesis 2:4–24

The biblical account of creation is itself a narrative story which includes elements of repetition and poetic description. This retelling expresses the sense of increasing abundance, joy and blessing in the biblical text. It also acts as an affirmation of our need to name and celebrate our day of rest.

Tell-it tips

This is a chain story. Phrases repeat and build up as the story progresses, giving it a gentle tongue-twisting feel. The story has a thoughtful, joyous tone and involves a strong element of rhythm and rhyme. It will require practice for a smooth and lyrical flow and should not be rushed.

Phrases and actions for everyone to say and/or do together appear in bold. Try them together briefly before the story begins.

Try it together

What a day God made (hands cupped out in front)!
And it was good (arms gradually lifted in praise)!

If you cup your hands out in front of you and pause before you say the first phrase, it will become a natural cue for participation whenever you do so during the story. The words 'very good' replace 'good' the last time the line is repeated.

I name this day. I call it blessed, a day for rest and thankfulness!

This opening line is repeated throughout the story and is also shown in bold. However, rather than practising the participation here, it is quite effective to let participation arise naturally as you go along. Invite folks to join you through your eye contact or a simple open hand gesture, as you feel appropriate.

Tell it together

I name this day. I call it blessed, a day for rest and thankfulness!
A day to remember the day God made everything from nothing, light from dark, a whole new world.

What a day God made (hands cupped out in front)!
And it was good (arms gradually lifted in praise)!

I name this day. I call it blessed, a day for rest and thankfulness!
A day to remember the day God made the earth below, the sky so blue, everything from nothing, light from dark, a whole new world.

What a day God made (hands cupped out in front)!
And it was good (arms gradually lifted in praise)!

I name this day. I call it blessed, a day for rest and thankfulness!
A day to remember the day God made rolling land and churning seas, grass and flowers and tall, tall trees, on the earth below the sky so blue, everything from nothing, light from dark, a whole new world.

What a day God made (hands cupped out in front)!
And it was good (arms gradually lifted in praise)!

I name this day. I call it blessed, a day for rest and thankfulness!
A day to remember the day God made day and night, the sun to wake by, the moon to sleep, the stars so bright over the land and the seas so deep, the grass, the flowers and the tall, tall trees on the earth below the sky so blue, everything from nothing, light from dark, a whole new world.

What a day God made (hands cupped out in front)!
And it was good (arms gradually lifted in praise)!

I name this day. I call it blessed, a day for rest and thankfulness!
A day to remember the day God made the birds that soar and the fish that swim, day and night, sun and moon and stars so bright over the land and the seas, the green, green grass, the flowers and the tall, tall trees on the earth below the sky so blue, everything from nothing, light from dark, a whole new world.

What a day God made (hands cupped out in front)!
And it was good (arms gradually lifted in praise)!

I name this day. I call it blessed, a day for rest and thankfulness!
A day to remember the day God made animals to hop and crawl and run, the birds to soar, the fish to swim, day and night, the moon and stars and sun so bright over the land, the seas, the grass, the flowers and the tall, tall trees on the earth below the sky so blue, everything from nothing, light from dark, a whole new world.

What a day God made (hands cupped out in front)!
And it was good (arms gradually lifted in praise)!

I name this day. I call it blessed, a day for rest and thankfulness!
A day to remember the day God made people like you and people like me, people like God! A man and woman to care for the animals that hop and crawl and run, the birds that soar, the fish that swim by day and night, under moon and stars and sun so bright over the land, the seas, the grass, the flowers and the tall, tall trees on the

earth below the sky so blue, everything from nothing, light from dark, a whole new world.

What a day God made (hands cupped out in front)!
And it was VERY good (arms gradually lifted in praise)!

I name this day. I call it blessed, a day for rest and thankfulness!
A day to remember the day God made to rest and be thankful for every day.

2

How things went wrong
The story of the fall

For your reflection: Genesis 3

The first people are given almost boundless freedom to enjoy the life that they are created for. The repercussions of their betrayal of God's trust are heartbreaking, not only for them but for all of humankind. The sense of brokenness in all that was good is the key emotion in this retelling.

Here I have brought the tree of life into focus (see also Revelation 22:2). There is also, in the biblical text, a reference to God as 'us' (Genesis 3:22) and the foreshadowing of Christ in God's plan of salvation (Genesis 3:15).

Tell-it tips

This story is written in rhyme but has the feel of a dramatic reading; aim for a reflective and sober tone and a gentle flow.

Try it together

Ask people to follow your lead naturally as you come to the actions. If you feel that doing the actions together will be distracting, simply ask your group to close their eyes and imagine what is happening in the story as you tell it.

Tell it together

Imagine the garden
Imagine Adam
and Eve
the hush of the rivers *(hush)*
the breeze in the trees *(wave arms gently)*
the tree of life stretching from fertile ground *(stretch up tall)*
full of fruit, so sweet and round *(bring your arms down to your sides
    in a wide circle)*
and the tree of the knowledge of good and evil *(foreboding
    finger wag)*
full of lush fruit, there too, in the middle *(point away from yourself)*.

Imagine the garden
Imagine Adam
and Eve
talking with God in the cool evening breeze *(wave arms gently)*
the sound of God's voice saying *(hand to ear)*
'Eat all that you please *(sweep arms out)*
from any of Eden's beautiful trees
except from the tree standing, there too, in the middle *(point
    to 'tree')*.
Don't eat of it, not even a little,
for it will bring death and the knowledge of evil' *(wag finger 'no')*.

Imagine the garden
Imagine Adam
Imagine Eve
Imagine the serpent that slithered into that tree *(slither with arm)*
Imagine Eve picking fruit nearby *(pick fruit)*
leaning in to the serpent who knew just how to lie *(hand to ear)*
Imagine the sound of its tempting hiss *(hissss)*

'Did God really say not to eat this?
You will be as wise as God if you do.
Try it and taste how delicious it is' *(crunch)*.

Imagine the garden
Imagine Adam
and Eve
after they'd eaten the fruit from that tree *(point to tree)*
after evil could do and evil could see
and how like God they could never be
after they knew they had broken God's trust *(shock)*
would toil on the earth, return to the dust *(point finger)*
Imagine their sorrow *(lower head)*
Imagine their shame *(shake head slowly)*
How they hid in the bushes *(hide)*
when God called them by name.

Imagine the garden
Imagine Adam
and Eve
Imagine God saying, 'Did you eat from that tree? *(point to tree)*
Is that why you are hiding from me?'

Imagine the garden
Imagine Adam
and Eve
Imagine the day God said they must leave
the hush of the rivers *(hush)*
the breeze in the trees *(wave arms gently)*
the tree of life stretching from fertile ground *(stretch up tall)*
full of fruit, so sweet and round *(bring your arms down to your sides
    in a wide circle)*
Imagine the angel with the flaming sword
that stands by the tree of life to keep guard.

3

Noah's nap

Noah builds a boat

For your reflection: Genesis 6—9

The biblical account of Noah's salvation (and that of his family) is wrapped up in the destruction of the world and everyone else in it. It recounts God's intent to rid the earth of evil and then recreate and repopulate it.

Despite this tragic context, there is also an immense joy and sturdy strength in Noah's journey to build the boat, survive the flood (with his menagerie of animals) and see the promise of God for their future in the first rainbow. I have tried to capture some of this joy in my retelling.

Tell-it tips

This story is strongly rhythmic and has a fun hoe-down kind of feel. You may want to tap the beat on your leg and tell it with an exaggerated drawl. There is even a group 'Yeeeee haaaa' at the end. That said, the story does gradually change pace and tone.

Toward its conclusion, use a softer, more natural tone of voice and make gentle effects with pauses and finger snaps before the rowdy final cheer.

Try it together

This is a call-and-repeat story. You will call a different phrase, with sounds and actions, at the end of each verse. Your group will then repeat it back. Phrases and actions for everyone to say and/or do together appear in bold. You may want to try these together before you begin. Alternatively, you can simply ask your group to repeat after you as you go along and nod them in naturally. This will maintain a level of suspense in the story.

The repeated phrases are as follows.

One, two, three, four *(slapping your thigh)*.
Let me hear your mighty roar *(wild animal roar and gesture)*.

One, two, three, four *(slapping your thigh)*,
Shut the door *(clap)*, **let it pour** *(slap knees and stomp feet)*.

One, two, three, four *(slapping your thigh)*.
Close your eyes *(head on hands)*, **let me hear you snore** *(all snore)*.

One *(snap finger)*… **two** *(snap finger)*…
three *(snap finger)*… **four** *(snap finger)*.

One, two, three, four *(slapping your thigh)*.
Let's lift our hands and praise the Lord *(lift and praise with hands)*.

Yeeeeee haaaaaa!

Tell it together

God told Noah to build a boat big and strong so it would float.
It was tall and long and wide. Lots of animals came inside.
One, two, three, four *(slapping your thigh)*.
Let me hear your mighty roar *(wild animal roar and gesture)*.
One, two, three, four *(slapping your thigh)*.
Let me hear your mighty roar *(wild animal roar and gesture)*.

Two by two they marched right in. Then the sky grew dark and dim.
When Noah's kin were safe on board, God shut the door and let
   it pour.
One, two, three, four *(slapping your thigh)*.
Shut the door *(clap)*, let it pour *(slap knees and stomp feet)*.
One, two, three, four *(slapping your thigh)*.
Shut the door *(clap)*, let it pour *(slap knees and stomp feet)*.

Tell me, friend, could you sleep sound, bobbing up as the rain
   came down?
Old Noah knew that they'd be safe on the boat God said to make.
One, two, three, four *(slapping your thigh)*.
Close your eyes *(head on hands)*, let me hear you snore *(snore)*.
One, two, three, four *(slapping your thigh)*.
Close your eyes *(head on hands)*, let me hear you snore *(all snore)*.

It rained and rained day after day, till everything was washed away.
It pittered. It pattered. It plipped… it plopped. Then one day… the
   rain done stopped.
One *(snap finger)*… two *(snap finger)*…
three *(snap finger)*… four *(snap finger)*.
One *(snap finger)*… two *(snap finger)*…
three *(snap finger)*… four *(snap finger)*.

When the world at last was dry, a rainbow spread across the sky.
They raised their hands and thanked the Lord for keeping them all
  safe on board.
One, two, three, four *(slapping your thigh)*.
Let's lift our hands and praise the Lord *(lift and praise with hands)*.
One, two, three, four *(slapping your thigh)*.
Let's lift our hands and praise the Lord *(lift and praise with hands)*.

Yeeeee haaaaaaa!
Yeeeee haaaaaaa!

4

I didn't mean to laugh
Sarah and Abraham have a son

For your reflection: Genesis 18 and 21

God's plan to restore what was lost in creation (first hinted at in the garden of Eden, Genesis 3:15) is set in motion through Abraham. The Saviour of the world will be one of his uncountable descendants.

Against this sweeping backdrop is the story of God's repeated promise to Abraham and his wife Sarah that they will have a son, despite their old age. This retelling captures both the longing for and celebration of the birth of Isaac, whose name means 'laughter'.

This story works best with older children, young people and adults.

Tell-it tips

This story has a thoughtful tone which rises to joy. Although it is written with a hint of rhyme, the rhyme is there to provide structure and a gentle rhythmic flow and should not be overt.

There is a single simple phrase for everyone to say together. Try it together briefly a few times before you begin your story. It appears in bold throughout. It will always follow the word 'and…' If you emphasise this in your practice (with an encouraging facial and/or hand gesture), people will know when to join in as you go along.

Try it together

Practise the phrase: 'and… **I didn't mean to laugh.'**

Tell it together

I didn't mean to listen in.
I didn't mean to laugh.
A baby—at my age? Impossible!
But that's what the angels said.
I didn't mean to listen in, and…
I didn't mean to laugh.

When we were spry and young,
God promised us a son,
more descendants than the stars or sand.
We waited long but no son came.
I didn't mean to make a sound, and…
I didn't mean to laugh.

There had been no swollen belly,
no kick, no infant cry.
There had been no tiny hand to hold
as sorrowed years went by.
I didn't mean to choke back tears, and…
I didn't mean to laugh.

How could it now be possible,
this promise from the past,
with silver hair and wrinkled hands?
A cruel joke, perhaps.
I didn't mean to doubt them, and…
I didn't mean to laugh.

'What is impossible for God?'
one of the angels asked.
'You'll have a son within the year
and then you'll really laugh!'
I didn't want dashed hopes again, and…
I didn't mean to laugh.

When Isaac was born, we laughed and laughed!
His name means 'laughter' too.
We redefined 'impossible'.
God's promises are true.

5

Bubble and boil

Jacob swindles Esau

For your reflection: Genesis 25 and 27

Isaac and Rebekah have twin sons, Jacob and Esau. The relationship between the two is fraught with parental favouritism, rivalry, deception and estrangement. In focus here is the loss of Esau's birthright to Jacob through an elaborate swindle, and the conflict it causes between their descendants.

This retelling captures a sense of foreboding within an almost farcical story.

Tell-it tips

This story is written in rhyme but has a foreboding tone and a strong sense of tension. It involves a chant with an action for everyone to say and do together. You will want to try it a few times before you begin.

Try it together

Practise saying together:
Bubble and boil, stirring the pot, Jacob wants what Esau's got!
(while pretending to stir stew).

Tell it together

When Rebekah and Isaac prayed for a son,
God gave them two rather than one.
'Double the trouble, double the joy!'
everyone said when they had their twin boys.
Esau came first, hairy and strong.
Jacob was born holding on.
Love stirred in each parent's heart,
but trouble was stewing right from the start.
Bubble and boil, stirring the pot, Jacob wants what Esau's got!

Esau loved outside, Jacob loved in.
Esau was burly. Jacob was thin.
Esau was loud, hair curly and red.
Jacob was sly, with dark hair on his head.
Esau loved hunting and brought home the meat
that Jacob loved cooking into a feast.
Isaac was proud and loved Esau the best.
Rebekah loved Jacob. It would stir up a mess.
Bubble and boil, stirring the pot, Jacob wants what Esau's got!

One day when Jacob was cooking some stew,
Esau came home and said, 'I'll have some too!'
Jacob was sneaky. Jacob was shrewd.
'You do look hungry…and I do have some food.
If you give me your birthright in future,' he said,
'I'll give you some stew and throw in some bread.'
Esau agreed his blessing away,
stirring up sorrow for another day.
Bubble and boil, stirring the pot, Jacob wants what Esau's got!

Many years later, the time had come
for old Isaac to bless his eldest son.
'Esau,' he said, 'this will be my last wish.
Hunt for some meat for my favourite dish.
Cook it yourself, just for us two.
Then I will pass God's blessing to you.'
Rebekah was listening, Rebekah was sly.
Rebekah stirred up a terrible lie.
Bubble and boil, stirring the pot, Jacob wants what Esau's got!

She found Jacob and filled him in quick,
moving on fast with their terrible trick.
'You kill two goats and I'll cook the feast.
You bring your father something tasty to eat.
We'll make you hairy like Esau,' she said.
'And your father will give you his blessing instead.'
And that is how Jacob came to wear
Esau's clothes and a skin of goat's hair.
Bubble and boil, stirring the pot, Jacob wants what Esau's got!

Jacob went to his father, food in hand.
'It's your son, Esau,' he lied just like he planned.
Isaac's eyes were now weak. He could no longer see.
'Come close, my son, and sit with me.
You sound like Jacob,' he said, reaching out.
'But you feel like Esau without a doubt.'
So Isaac blessed his youngest son,
not knowing that he had blessed the wrong one.
Bubble and boil, stirring the pot, Jacob wants what Esau's got!

Oh the hatred that stirred, the cry unrepeated
when Esau discovered that he had been cheated!
'I will murder my brother,' he stewed in his anger.
'Run, son,' cried their mother. 'Your life is in danger!
Run to your uncle till Esau forgets.'
But it would be years before the two brothers met.
What happened when Jacob went far away?
We'll let that story simmer for another day.

6

A colourful story
Joseph forgives his brothers

For your reflection: Genesis 37; 39—45 and 50

Jacob has twelve sons. Favouritism towards Joseph sparks such jealousy that his ten older brothers plot to kill him. Thus begins the saga of how Joseph is sold into slavery and rises to become the second most powerful man in Egypt, next to Pharaoh. When a famine sweeps across the region, Joseph's brothers travel to Egypt in search of food. This sets the scene for their parallel journey of reunion, forgiveness and reconciliation.

This retelling captures the breadth of the story (though not every detail), the depth of Joseph's faith in God and his determination to trust God's plan.

Tell-it tips

This is an active story, fun and quick-paced. Participants stand up and sit down on key words. If this proves tricky for some (or even the majority), ask them to raise and lower their hands instead. You will want to prepare the story beforehand. Key words appear in block capitals so that you may emphasise them easily as you tell it.

The story can be told in three parts, each one ending on a bit of a cliff-hanger, or it can be told as one whole.

Try it together

- Those who are wearing the colour mentioned stand up and sit down again quickly (or raise and lower their hands).
- Everyone stands up and hugs themselves on the word 'COAT'.
- Only those who have 'silver' hair stand up or raise their hands on the word 'SILVER'.
- You will say the word 'WHITE' once (during the quick-fire summary) and it will be a signal for everyone to sit down.

Have a quick practice, calling a few colours and the word 'COAT', before you start.

Tell it together

Part 1

Jacob had a lot of sons, but Joseph was his favourite one. So Jacob made him a colourful COAT. Joseph's brothers were GREEN with envy.

One night, Joseph's sleep was deep. He told his brothers about the dream he had. 'We were bundles of GOLDen grain and you all bowed down to me!' he said.

His brothers saw RED. 'This dream will not come true. We will never bow to you.'

Joseph had another dream. 'This time, you were SILVER stars when you bowed to me,' he said. The brothers saw RED.

From early morn until the day grew dim, Joseph's brothers hated him.

One day, they saw Joseph coming in his COAT. They were GREEN with envy and RED with rage. They took the COAT and threw him into a BLACK pit. Joseph felt BLUE.

Then they took him out of the BLACK pit and sold him to slave traders for 20 SILVER coins.

'Joseph is dead,' they said to their dad and gave him the COAT as proof.

Jacob felt BLUE and began to cry. Oh, how the brothers regretted their lie. Days were BLACK and nights were grim because of what they'd done to him.

Part 2

When Joseph finally fell asleep, his eyes were RED but his sleep was deep. Even though he was in jail, he knew that God would never fail.

The king of Egypt had dreams too—BLACK dreams.

'Tell me what my dreams are about and I'll let you out!' said the king.

And that's how Joseph came to know about the crops that wouldn't grow.

'For seven years there will be GOLDen grain in plenty. Then for seven years you won't have any! You're going to need a GOLDen plan to feed the people of your land,' said Joseph.

The king looked BLUE and then he grinned. 'Joseph. My plan is you! You can tell us what to do!'

So while the crops were GREEN and good, Joseph stored up lots of food. When the crops were BLACK and bad, he shared from the plenty that they had. Joseph was treated like a king. He was in charge of everything! From early morn until the day grew dim, Joseph trusted God's plan for him.

Part 3

When Joseph's brothers went to sleep, they felt BLUE. They were hungry. Their father was, too. There was only one thing left to do. They went to Egypt far away. That's how they came to see Joseph one day.

It had been a long time. Joseph looked like a king! Joseph knew them, but they did not know him. They bowed down on their knees.

'We have come to buy food,' they said. 'Can you help us, please?'

Joseph was amazed at this sight. He remembered his dreams. His dreams were right! He filled their sacks with GOLDen grain. When they needed more, they came back again.

Joseph found out that his brothers felt BLUE about what they had done. They were no longer RED with anger or GREEN with envy.

Joseph couldn't help but tell. 'It's me—your brother Joseph! I'm alive and well.'

There was lots of laughter and many tears.

Joseph said, 'You hurt me, it's true. But God used it for good. Now I can help you. I choose to be thankful. I choose to forgive. Bring Father with you and come here to live!'

From early morn until the day grew dim, Joseph's family were glad God had a plan for them.

Quick-fire summary

Joseph had a cool COAT. His brothers were GREEN, saw RED and threw him into a BLACK pit. Joseph was BLUE, sold for SILVER but stored GOLDen grain. His brothers were forgiven and everything was all WHITE!

7

The basket baby

Moses is born

For your reflection: Exodus 1:22—2:10

The descendants of the Israelites who migrated to Egypt become many and strong. A pharaoh rises to power who fears that they may take over, so he turns them into slaves. The people cry out to God to free them, and God sends Moses to do just that.

Moses is born while Pharaoh's population control policy is in force, to kill newborn Israelite boys. This retelling captures some of the drama as well as the divine irony: Moses is rescued by Pharaoh's own daughter and is raised as an Egyptian prince with the help of his own birth mother.

Tell-it tips

This story is written in rhyme and includes a lyric from a well-known nursery song. Its tone, however, is not light-hearted. Aim to capture the sinister and ironic context of the story and, of course, the sense of joyful completion.

The lyric is spoken rather than sung. You will want to try it together before you begin.

Try it together

Practise saying these lines together.

Hush little baby *(mime rocking the baby).*
Don't say a thing *(finger to mouth in a whisper).*

Hush little baby *(mime rocking the baby).*
Don't you cry *(finger to mouth in a whisper).*

Tell it together

Once upon a wicked time there lived a wicked king
who was wicked to God's people and made them slaves to him.
He hated that God's people were living in his land—
feared how many there might one day be—so he devised a
    wicked plan.

'Throw all their baby boys in the river Nile!'
said the wicked king with a wicked smile.

Now a slave woman named Jochabed had a sweet little son.
She sang a sweet song all night long.
'Hush little baby *(mime rocking the baby).*
Don't say a thing *(finger to mouth in a whisper).*
We must keep you a secret from the nasty king.'

But the baby got bigger as babies always do.
Now what was his sweet mother to do?
'Hush little baby *(mime rocking the baby).*
Don't say a thing *(finger to mouth in a whisper).*
We must give your sweet mother time to think.'

She made a basket and tucked him safe inside.
Then she hid the basket by the riverside.
'Hush little baby *(mime rocking the baby)*.
Don't you cry *(finger to mouth in a whisper)*.
Your big sister Miriam keeps an eye close by.'

Now a pretty princess with a pretty smile
often took a bath in the river Nile.
She saw the basket bobbing by the riverside.
She saw the bitty baby tucked up safe inside.
'Hush little baby *(mime rocking the baby)*.
Don't you cry *(finger to mouth in a whisper)*.'
She sighed, 'I will love you. I will not let you die!'

Miriam saw how the princess loved her little brother.
'You will need some help,' she said. 'I will go and get my mother.'
Now a slave woman named Jochabed held her sweet little son
and sang a sweet song all night long.
'Hush little Moses *(mime rocking the baby)*. God knows everything.
You are now a prince in the palace of a king!'

8

Bondage and chains
Moses kills an Egyptian

For your reflection: Exodus 5

Moses knows that he is an Israelite by birth and he has compassion for his enslaved people. In the story, he murders an Egyptian slave-driver and runs away. The consequences of his act will eventually lead him into a life-changing encounter with the living God. This will, in turn, set him off on his journey to save his people from their slavery.

This story captures the relentless drudgery of bondage and the cries of God's people for freedom. It also touches on some of the themes in the book of Exodus—that God cares about the suffering of his people, that God has a plan and a purpose for his people, and that God calls and uses the least likely people. It can be used on its own or as a companion piece to the next story, 'Our God saves'.

This story works best with older primary school children, young people and adults. Be aware that the subject matter may be difficult for some.

Tell-it tips

This retelling will be most effective if you divide your group into three. Each small group is given one of three simple chants; one to be repeated after each verse in the story. After the last verse, all chants are repeated together at the same time.

Try it together

Divide your group into three. Give each group an opportunity to practise their chant once through before you begin.

Group 1

**Bondage and chains
day after day
making bricks from straw and clay.**

Group 2

**Crack of the whip
day after day
making bricks from straw and clay.**

Group 3

**Weep and pray
day after day
making bricks from straw and clay.**

Tell it together

The king of Egypt was nasty and cruel
in the way he chose to rule.
He put God's people into bondage and chains,
cracked the whip and made them slaves.

(Group 1)

**Bondage and chains
day after day
making bricks from straw and clay.**

When little Prince Moses became a man,
he went out to have a look at the land.
He saw the way God's people were used;
saw a slave-man being abused.

(Group 2)

Crack of the whip
day after day
making bricks from straw and clay.

He killed the master who beat on the man
and buried him quickly under the sand.
He ran away to avoid arrest
and made a new life in the wilderness.

(Group 3)

Weep and pray
day after day
making bricks from straw and clay.

Day after day, the years went by.
Day after day, God heard their cries.

Gesture to each small group to repeat their chants in turn. Then finish
by gesturing to them to chant all together at the same time.

Bondage and chains
day after day
making bricks from straw and clay.

Crack of the whip
day after day
making bricks from straw and clay.

Weep and pray
day after day
making bricks from straw and clay.

God had a plan to set them all free.
He would use Moses—and so they would be
free from the crack of the whip every day,
free from their weeping, bondage and chains.

9

our God saves
Miriam sings a song of praise

For your reflection: Exodus 15

The story of the exodus is as amazing as it is exciting. God chooses Moses to lead the Israelites out of slavery and into the wilderness to Mt Sinai. There, God enters into a covenant with them, promising to be faithful to them and give them a land of their own. They are to be faithful to and serve God alone. They are given laws (including the ten commandments) and plans for building a tabernacle, so that God can live among them.

This retelling combines the story of their flight from Egypt and their Red Sea crossing with the joy of Miriam's song of praise—which they all joined in together as a celebration of their freedom. The story can be used on its own or as a companion-piece to 'Bondage and chains'.

This story works best with older children, young people and adults. Be aware of the sensitivities that may exist around the subject of violence.

Tell-it tips

This retelling is pacy and celebratory in tone.

Try it together

Everybody repeats this chant together between verses.

Sing to God, day after day:
God is great! Our God saves!

Tell it together

The king of Egypt was nasty and cruel,
but we know that our God rules!
He heard our cries when we were slaves,
and rescued us, for our God saves!

Moses said, 'Set God's people free!'
But Pharaoh said, 'No! They belong to me!'
He worked us harder day after day,
but God rescued us, for our God saves!

Sing to God, day after day:
God is great! Our God saves!

Moses said, 'Let God's people go!'
But hard-hearted Pharaoh kept saying, 'No!'
The river ran blood; there were many plagues.
God rescued us, for our God saves!

Death passed over and took their first sons,
but we were safe—every one.
Pharaoh said, 'Go! This very day!'
God rescued us, for our God saves!

Sing to God, day after day:
God is great! Our God saves!

We left in a hurry, took all we could pack.
But Pharaoh soon wanted to bring us all back.

'After them!' he shouted. 'Don't let them get away!'
But God rescued us, for our God saves!

All Pharaoh's armies and all Pharaoh's men
were not enough to catch us again.
God provided a way of escape,
God rescued us, for our God saves!

Sing to God, day after day:
God is great! Our God saves!

We walked on dry land, a path through the sea.
Then the waters crashed down on our enemies.
We were amazed! We still sing God's praise!
God rescued us, for our God saves!

10

Grumble, grump and groan
Wandering in the desert

For your reflection: Exodus 16:1–16; 17:1–7; 40:34–38

The Israelites set out to the promised land through the desert. They are quick to complain and slow to ask for God's help or thank him for his miraculous provision. Their lack of trust is evident when they get to the border but refuse to enter. Joshua and Caleb, two of twelve scouts sent into the promised land to report back, are confident about taking it. The rest of the Israelites, however, believe those who are fearful. As a consequence, everyone must wander in the desert for a further 40 years, until most of the adults who left Egypt are dead.

This retelling is light-hearted in tone but captures the relentless nature of the desert-wandering and of the complaining.

Tell-it tips

Keep the telling light and jaunty. You will want to try the refrains together before you start. Let people know that the first refrain will be used in the first two verses and the second refrain in the last two verses. You will point to them when it's time for them to join in the story.

Try it together

Try the refrains together before you start.

Mumble, mump and moan.
Mumble, mump and moan.

Grumble, grump and groan.
Grumble, grump and groan.

Tell it together

God promised his people a new land, a land to call their own.
But all they ever seemed to do was mumble, mump and moan.
Mumble, mump and moan.
Mumble, mump and moan.
All they ever seemed to do was mumble, mump and moan.

'We're hungry! We're tired! We're thirsty!' they whined. 'We should
    have stayed at home.'

'God takes care of us every day,' said Moses. 'How quickly
    you forget.
We have manna, meat and water. There's no need to fret!
We're going to a new land, a land to call our own!
Give your thanks to God! Don't mumble, mump and moan.
Mumble, mump and moan.
Mumble, mump and moan
Give your thanks to God! Don't mumble, mump and moan.'

God saved them from their slavery, never left them alone.
But all they ever seemed to do was grumble, grump and groan.
Grumble, grump and groan.
Grumble, grump and groan.
All they ever seemed to do was grumble, grump and groan.

'How long until we get there?' they whined. 'We just want to go
    back home.'

'God leads us every day,' said Moses. 'How quickly you forget.
God is in the cloud and fire before us. There's no need to fret!
We're going to a new land, a land to call our own!
Give your thanks to God! Don't grumble, grump and groan.
Grumble, grump and groan.
Grumble, grump and groan.
Give your thanks to God! Don't grumble, grump and groan.'

God was patient with his people everywhere they roamed.
God is patient with us too, when we mumble, mump and moan.
Give your thanks to God! Don't grumble, grump and groan.

ll

The red rope
Rahab monologue

For your reflection: Joshua 2:1–13; 3:9–17; 6:17–25

When the Israelites finally enter the promised land, they do so miraculously. God makes a dry path through a river, reminiscent of the miracle of the Red Sea. Moses has died and Joshua is now their leader. Their first battle will be with the people of Jericho, who are protected by the walls of their city.

Before this battle, Joshua sends two spies into Jericho. They are nearly discovered and are helped to escape by Rahab. In return, they promise to spare her and her family when they come back to take Jericho. Rahab is known for her great faith and her place in the lineage of Jesus Christ.

This story works best with older children, young people and adults. Be aware of the sensitivities that may exist around the subject of war.

Tell-it tips

This retelling is a monologue from Rahab's point of view.

Try it together

Encourage everyone to imagine what it might have been like to be inside Jericho as the Israelites surrounded the city.

Tell it together

Everyone in Jericho was nervous. We knew that God had saved his people in Egypt. We had heard how the waters of the river swept back to let them cross into our land, this land that God had promised them. We knew that they would come. I knew it. I had been waiting a long time, but I knew that they would come.

I had seen two of their spies myself. I hid them on the roof when their presence in the city was discovered. I helped them escape through my window and scamper down the walls. But first we made a deal.

I would hang a red rope from my window. They'd see it and save my life as I had saved theirs. They would save my family too. As their army gathered below, I hoped that they would keep their promise. I hoped they would even remember it.

It was a strange way to win a battle. They had no weapons. They just followed their trumpeters and a beautiful golden box. Every day for six days, they marched silently around our walls once and stopped.

People began to wonder what they had been so afraid of.

But on the seventh day it was different. They marched seven times around. This time, when they stopped, we heard the trumpets blasting and people shouting. Suddenly, the walls began to crumble and fall around us.

It was chaos! I was afraid. But as the army claimed the city, they saw the red rope and rescued us. That is how I came to be among them, part of them, and believing in their God.

12

Samson's Delilah dilemma
The story of Samson

For your reflection: Judges 16:4–30

The book of Judges is full of gut-wrenching stories about what happens to Israel after Joshua dies. Despite the grave consequences of their repeated rebellion, God continues to love and help his people—often through the aid of appointed judges who are more anti-hero than hero.

Samson is a case in point. He is Israel's weak-willed strong man who ends up sapped of his God-given strength and captured by the Philistines when his hair is cut by Delilah. Every decision he makes seems ill-motivated. Yet God uses him to help Israel defeat their enemies.

This retelling, though light-hearted, definitely has a serious core.

This story works best with older children, young people and adults. Be aware that the subject matter may be sensitive for some.

Tell-it tips

This is a call-and-response story with actions. You will say the key words and the group will respond by repeating the words and doing the actions. You will want to try it together before you begin.

Try it together

Sad, **sad** *(make a sad face and trace tears down your cheeks)*
Glad, **glad** *(make a happy face and trace a smile on your lips)*
Big, **big** *(mime 'big' with your hands in the air)*
Strong, **strong** *(arms out like a strong man)*
Long, **long** *(mime brushing hair)*
Bad, **bad** *(make a snarly face)*
Tad, **tad** *(mime 'tiny' with your pointer finger and thumb)*

Tell it together

A SAD, **SAD** woman felt so alone. She and her husband had no child to call their own. Then an angel came with GLAD, **GLAD** news. 'You are going to have a son. It's true! He will help to save your people from their enemies—the Philistines and their BAD, **BAD** ways. He will vow to serve God from his earliest days. As a sign of this vow, you must never cut his hair. Remember how God answered your BIG, **BIG** prayer.'

The SAD, **SAD** woman was filled with joy on the GLAD, **GLAD** day she gave birth to a boy. His name was Samson and he grew and grew, loved by his mother and his father too.

Indeed, it came as no surprise when Samson grew in strength and size. Samson was such a STRONG, **STRONG** man that he once killed a lion with his STRONG, **STRONG** hands. His strength came from God and the vow he did swear never to cut his LONG, **LONG** hair.

The Philistines were fearsome, always up for a fight, but they couldn't beat Samson, try as they might. Their hatred for him grew and grew, because he protected his people as he vowed to do. The Philistines needed a BIG, **BIG** plan in a BAD, **BAD** way to beat this STRONG, **STRONG** man some day.

Now Samson was not always good, didn't always do the things he should. For though he was a STRONG, **STRONG** man, he was also weak and went off plan. His pride in himself grew and grew and he often did just what he wanted to. He was easily flattered and led astray and made a BAD, **BAD** choice one SAD, **SAD** day.

Her name was Delilah and he thought her delicious—even though he should have been a TAD, **TAD** suspicious. For the BAD, **BAD** Philistines bribed her to spy while they hid themselves in a room nearby.

'Now Delilah,' they said, 'here's the BIG, **BIG** plan. Find out why Samson is such a STRONG, **STRONG** man. Discover his secret and we will pay, for we want to tie him up and take him away.'

So that night, when Delilah brushed Samson's LONG, **LONG** hair, she looked into his eyes with her own so fair.

'Do tell me your secret,' she said, 'for you know you can. Why are you such a STRONG, **STRONG** man?'

Samson thought it a TAD, **TAD** awry, so he told Delilah a BIG, **BIG** lie.

'Seven new bow strings tied up tight would cause me to lose my STRONG, **STRONG** might.'

Samson slept. Delilah tied him up tight. The BAD, **BAD** Philistines hid out of sight.

'Samson! You're in danger!' she cried out in dread. Samson snapped the strings and jumped out of bed.

His BIG, **BIG** secret had not been discovered. The BAD, **BAD** Philistines stayed undercover.

Delilah was cross. 'You tricked me!' she cried. 'Why did you tell me such a BIG, **BIG** lie? Do tell me the truth. You know you can. Why are you such a STRONG, **STRONG** man?'

Samson thought this question a TAD, **TAD** sly, so he told Delilah another BIG, **BIG** lie.

'Brand new ropes tied up tight will make me lose my STRONG, **STRONG** might.'

Samson slept. Delilah tied him up tight. The BAD, **BAD** Philistines hid out of sight.

'Samson! You're in danger!' she cried out in dread. But he snapped the ropes and jumped out of bed.

His BIG, **BIG** secret had not been discovered. The BAD, **BAD** Philistines stayed undercover.

Delilah looked hurt and gave a SAD, **SAD** sigh. 'Why did you tell me such a BIG, **BIG** lie? Do tell me the truth. You know you can. Why are you such a STRONG, **STRONG** man?'

Samson thought it TAD, **TAD** amiss, so he told a BIG, **BIG** lie like this.

'If my LONG, **LONG** hair is braided tight, I will lose my STRONG, **STRONG** might.'

Samson slept. Delilah braided his LONG, **LONG** hair. Samson woke up stronger than ever!

His BIG, **BIG** secret had not been discovered. The BAD, **BAD** Philistines stayed undercover.

Day after day Delilah cried. 'Why do you tell me such BIG, **BIG** lies? If you love me, you'll tell me. You know you can. Why are you such a STRONG, **STRONG** man?'

Samson grew tired of her pestering and finally told her everything.

'My strength comes from God and the vow I did swear never to cut my LONG, **LONG** hair. If it is shaved, my strength is undone. I'd be as weak as anyone.'

As Samson slept that SAD, **SAD** night, the BAD, **BAD** Philistines hid out of sight. GLAD, **GLAD** Delilah cut his LONG, **LONG** hair and shouted out into the night-time air.

'Samson! You're in danger!' she feigned in fright. But this time Samson was too weak to fight.

What a SAD, **SAD** day when the BAD, **BAD** Philistines took Samson away. They blinded his eyes, they bound him in chains, threw him in prison and made him grind grain. Day after day they taunted and jeered the man they once feared. But, a little each day his hair grew and grew. Hardly anyone noticed or thought what he might do.

SAD, **SAD** Samson was put on display in the Philistine temple one BIG, **BIG** day. Thousands were gathered to poke fun at his shame but Samson the powerless called out in God's name. 'One last time—let your strength be mine.'

He pushed on the pillars, down came the walls and Samson died with the Philistines.

13

A sleepless night
Samuel listens

For your reflection: 1 Samuel 3

Samuel is called by God to be the spiritual leader of his people. When he grows old, the people decide they want a king, just like other nations. However, the point of God's covenant with the Israelites is that they are not like other nations. They are God's people, and God is their king. Yet God honours their request. Samuel will be instrumental in the anointing of their first two kings.

This retelling focuses on the beginning of Samuel's life. His mother, Hannah, dedicates him to God's service and he goes to live under the care of the priest, Eli. Here, Samuel learns to listen to God's voice.

Tell-it tips

This call-and-response story has a sleepy lullaby feel. It is reflective in tone and involves a gentle element of rhythm and rhyme. It will require practice for a smooth and lyrical flow and should not be rushed.

You will give the cues verbally, and gestures for everyone to do together appear in bold. Try them together with your group before the story begins.

Try it together

Invite everyone to do the following actions together on cue.

- Sleepy eyes *(head on hands, eyes closed)*
- Sleep so softly came *(gentle snoring)*
- Thought he heard *(hand to ear)*
- Here I am *(hands out with palms up)*

Note: Pause after each cue and give everyone time to respond and settle before moving on. This will mimic what is actually happening in the story.

Tell it together

Young Samuel lived in God's house and helped Eli the priest all day. He learned to love God and serve others, to listen and to pray.

One night, as he closed his sleepy eyes *(head on hands, eyes closed)* and sleep so softly came *(gentle snoring)*,
he thought he heard *(hand to ear)* old Eli calling out his name.

Samuel went to Eli. 'Here I am,' *(hands out with palms up)* he said.
'I didn't call you,' Eli replied. 'It's time you were in bed.'

As Samuel closed his sleepy eyes *(head on hands, eyes closed)* and sleep so softly came *(gentle snoring)*,
he thought he heard *(hand to ear)*, a second time, old Eli call his name.

Samuel went to Eli. 'Here I am,' *(hands out with palms up)* he said.
'I didn't call you,' Eli replied. 'Please go back to bed.'

As Samuel closed his sleepy eyes *(head on hands, eyes closed)*
and sleep so softly came *(gentle snoring)*,
he thought he heard *(hand to ear)*, a third time, old Eli call
    his name.

Samuel went to Eli. 'Here I am,' *(hands out with palms up)* he said.
This time Eli understood. 'I didn't get you out of bed,' he said.
'It is God who calls you near.
Next time, when he calls your name, tell him that you hear.'

Samuel closed his sleepy eyes *(head on hands, eyes closed)*
and when God called his name again,
Samuel heard *(hand on ear)* and said, 'Here I am! *(hands out with
    palms up)*. I am listening!'

14

David's giant problem
David and Goliath

For your reflection: 1 Samuel 17

God chooses Saul to be the first king of Israel, but Saul soon rebels against God. David is anointed as his successor. The relationship between the murderously jealous Saul and the increasingly popular David forms the heart of many stories. So too does the friendship between David and Saul's son, Jonathan.

David's imperfections and experiences are very human. They also affirm how God loves us and works with us just as we are. Here we meet David the giant-slayer and can glimpse a bit of why God called David 'a man after my own heart' (Acts 13:22).

Tell-it tips

This story works well in a variety of ways and involves three chants. You can tell it together as a whole group, with everyone repeating the same phrases and gestures together, or you can divide the group into three: Goliaths, Davids and Soldiers. It also works well as an impromptu drama: choose a volunteer Goliath and David to join you at the front and have everyone else as soldiers.

The chants and actions appear in bold in the story. You will want to let each group try their chant together before you begin. It can be fun to vary the pitch of your voice or accent as you do so. Actions will be picked up naturally as you go along. You do the action first and gesture to your group to repeat it with you.

Try it together

Goliaths

I'm the biggest giant you ever did see *(stomp)*.
None of you is brave enough to come and fight me *(put your thumbs in your ears, wiggle your fingers and say 'na, na, na, na, na' in a taunting manner)*.

Soldiers

That guy is big *(show muscles)*; **that guy is grim** *(face of fear)*!
None of us is brave enough to go and fight him *(knock knees and chatter teeth)*!

Davids

Put your trust in God. Just you wait and see.
Put your trust in God to defeat your enemy!

Tell it together

Goliath was the mightiest, frightiest giant that God's army had ever seen. He wore a giant helmet *(tap head)*, a giant breastplate *(tap chest)*, giant shoes *(stomp feet)* and held a giant sword *(wave 'sword')*. He had a giant voice *(na, na, na, na, na)* and a giant streak of mean *(beat chest and stomp feet)*.

Every day Goliath shouted:
I'm the biggest giant you ever did see *(stomp)*.
None of you is brave enough to come and fight me *(na, na, na, na, na)*.

And every day the soldiers said:

That guy is big *(show muscles)*; that guy is grim *(face of fear)*!
None of us is brave enough to go and fight him *(knock knees and chatter teeth)*!

King Saul was not impressed. But what could he do? It all seemed so hopeless!

Now David was a shepherd boy. He was young and small but that didn't matter to him at all. One day he heard Goliath shout:

I'm the biggest giant you ever did see *(stomp)*.
None of you is brave enough to come and fight me *(na, na, na, na, na)*.

And he heard the soldiers say:

That guy is big *(show muscles)*; that guy is grim *(face of fear)*!
None of us is brave enough to go and fight him *(knock knees and chatter teeth)*!

This annoyed David. 'Will no one fight?' he asked. 'Are you all asleep? God saved me from bears when I looked after sheep. Goliath may be mighty, but God is mightier still. If no one else will fight him, I surely will!'

Put your trust in God. Just you wait and see.
Put your trust in God to defeat your enemy!

King Saul thought it impossible. The soldiers laughed. But David was determined.

The king gave David his armour, but it would have fit a giant *[sell this wordplay to the audience with a big wink]*. The helmet was too big *(tap head)*, the breastplate was too big *(tap chest)*, the shoes were too big *(stomp feet)* and the sword was too heavy *(wave 'sword')*.

David gave the armour back and took out his shepherd's sling. 'You can't beat Goliath with that silly thing,' said the king.

David said:

Put your trust in God. Just you wait and see.
Put your trust in God to defeat your enemy!

And off he went to fetch stones and face Goliath. It only took one. David faced the giant and swung his sling round his head. The stone hit Goliath and he fell down—dead.

God's army cheered. God's enemies ran away. God is the mightiest and the greatest—and David trusted him that day.

Everybody joins in with David's chant:
Put your trust in God. Just you wait and see.
Put your trust in God to defeat your enemy!

15

Elijah and the ravens
Elijah is fed by ravens

For your reflection: 1 Kings 17:1–5

Solomon (known for his exceptional wisdom) succeeds David as king. He builds the first temple, used as a centre for worship for 400 years before it is destroyed. However, Solomon also allows his large harem of foreign wives and concubines to turn his heart to other gods. This idolatry results in shattered peace and a divided kingdom—northern and southern.

Ahab is a notoriously wicked king from the north. His wife, Jezebel, kills most of God's prophets and imports her own—prophets of Baal, the god of rain. Hence, God punishes Israel with three years of drought. This ends in a contest between God's prophet, Elijah, and the prophets of Baal, in which God brings down fire, followed soon afterwards by rain.

In this retelling, Elijah is sent to warn King Ahab about the coming drought and is then sent into hiding for his own safety. There, he is fed by ravens (usually scavengers of death and regarded as unclean by law).

Tell-it tips

This story is a mini monologue and is reflective in tone. It includes a simple verse to say and hand gestures for everyone to do together, before and after the story. You will want to try it together a few times until it runs smoothly.

Try it together

Before the story

Here are the birds that fly overhead *(hook thumbs and make a bird to fly overhead, backs of hands facing out)*.

Here is the raven that brings me bread *(gently swoop 'bird' down across your body; finish with palms up as if making an offering)*.

After the story

Thanks for the birds that fly overhead *(hook thumbs and make a bird to fly overhead, backs of hands facing out)*.

Thanks for the raven that brings me bread *(gently swoop 'bird' down across your body; finish with palms up as if making an offering)*.

Tell it together

Here are the birds that fly overhead *(hook thumbs and make a bird to fly overhead, backs of hands facing out)*.

Here is the raven that brings me bread *(gently swoop 'bird' down across your body; finish with palms up as if making an offering)*.

The first time I saw the ravens, I was nervous; they were scavengers of the dead, unclean by law. I heard them gathering, felt the force of their flapping wings as they circled above me. Then I remembered God's promise—his plan to save my life.

There would be no rain for three years, not until God chose to send it. This was the message I had brought to wicked King Ahab and his wicked queen. They had rejected the one true God, built a temple to Baal and led God's people away from him. God would show them just who was real.

Ahab was raging! I knew he would kill me. But first, he'd have to find me. 'Go and hide by the river,' God said. 'You will have water to drink and everything else you need.' And I did.

Every morning and evening, one by one, the ravens swooped near. I soon became comforted by their presence. Sometimes they dropped meat, sometimes bread, but it was always enough. God had a plan to save my life from Ahab and the famine. I stayed safe by the brook until it too ran dry.

Thanks for the birds that fly overhead *(hook thumbs and make a bird to fly overhead, backs of hands facing out)*.

Thanks for the raven that brings me bread *(gently swoop 'bird' down across your body; finish with palms up as if making an offering)*.

16

Just enough
The miracle of the widow's jar

For your reflection: 1 Kings 17:8–16

When the brook that has been sustaining Elijah dries up, God sends him to a widow in Zarephath. She and her son are at the end of their own resources when he arrives and she fears that there is not enough to share. Elijah performs his first miracle there: the widow's jar of flour and jug of oil do not run out until the drought is over. In a later miracle, the widow's son dies and Elijah brings him back to life.

This retelling focuses on the miracle of having just enough to sustain us over and over again.

Tell-it tips

This story is a mini monologue and is reflective in tone. It includes a simple verse to say and hand gestures for everyone to do together, before and after the story. You will want to try it together a few times before you begin.

Try it together

Before the story

This is the jar that fills up again *(cup hands in front of you)*
when there's too much sun *(raise hands to the air)* **and not enough
  rain** *(hands down again, making rain with fingers)*.

After the story

Thanks for the jar that fills up again *(cup hands in front of you)*
when there's too much sun *(raise hands to the air)* **and not enough
rain** *(hands down again, making rain with fingers).*

Tell it together

This is the jar that fills up again *(cup hands in front of you)*
when there's too much sun *(raise hands to the air)* **and not enough
rain** *(hands down again, making rain with fingers).*

There was too much sun and not enough rain. There was not
enough grain to make bread. There was not enough water to drink.

God sent Elijah to me for help. I was out gathering firewood when
he came. We were both hungry and thirsty, and so was my son.

'May I have some water and some bread?' asked Elijah.

'I don't have any bread,' I said. 'I have just enough flour and oil to
make one last meal. Then my son and I will be dead.'

'God will take care of you,' Elijah promised. 'Do as I ask and you will
find that you always have just enough, time after time.'

So I gave Elijah some water and baked him some bread. The jar of
flour should have been empty, but it wasn't. The jug of oil should
have been empty, but it wasn't.

From that day on until there was just enough rain, I had just enough
flour and oil, over and over again.

Thanks for the jar that fills up again *(cup hands in front of you)*
when there's too much sun *(raise hands to the air)* **and not enough
rain** *(hands down again, making rain with fingers).*

17

Again and again
Jeremiah and the fall of Jerusalem

For your reflection: Jeremiah 40 and 52

Jeremiah, the prophet, was an eyewitness to unimaginable tragedy in Israel's history—Jerusalem's fall at the hands of the Babylonians. People are slaughtered and survivors taken off in bondage; Jerusalem is burning, the temple in ruins. *And* he had seen it coming for 40 years, warning God's people, telling them that it didn't need to end this way.

This retelling captures Jeremiah's despair.

This story is best for older children, young people and adults. Be aware of the sensitivities that may exist around the subject of war.

Tell-it tips

This monologue is sombre in tone. There is a simple phrase repeated throughout. You will want to try it together once before you begin. If you pause briefly and give a gentle nod or gesture before the phrase each time it appears, your group will naturally know when to join in.

Try it together

This phrase is repeated throughout the story. Try it once together before you begin.

Again and again

Tell it together

I cried **again and again** when my people wouldn't believe me. I warned them **again and again** about what would happen. I told them that it wasn't too late, **again and again**. God would protect us from our enemies if we trusted him.

'You must surrender to the Babylonians,' I said to the king **again and again**, 'or you and your family will die.' But **again and again** he wouldn't listen. And now the city was on fire!

There was chaos everywhere. The temple was looted, walls crumbled around us, people were screaming **again and again**. The king's sons were killed in front of him. Then he himself was blinded and taken off to die. Almost everyone but the poorest was taken prisoner—even me. The chains around my wrists and ankles rattled and clanked **again and again**.

A captain in the Babylonian guard kept looking in my direction, **again and again**, as if he recognised me. When he came up to me, I was worried.

'I recognise you,' he said. 'You are Jeremiah.' I held my breath. 'You told your people that this would happen, **again and again**. You believed what your God said **again and again**. Our king says that you are free to go. You can come and live with us or you can stay here.'

I chose to remain with those who were poor—weeping **again and again** in the rubble of Jerusalem.

18

Day in, day out
Daniel is saved from the lions

For your reflection: Daniel 6

One of the Bible's most popular stories involves Daniel, a godly nobleman forced into Babylonian exile. Daniel is known to be a praying man of integrity and has a good relationship with King Darius. When Daniel becomes one of the king's top officials, the other officials plot to kill him. They shrewdly persuade the king to order everyone to pray only to him or be executed. They catch Daniel praying to God and throw him to the lions.

The king is upset, but the edict must stand. Daniel spends the night with the lions, but is protected by an angel. The next morning, the king rushes to the den to find that Daniel is still alive. He releases Daniel and throws his accusers into the den instead.

This retelling captures the drama of the story, the faithfulness of Daniel and the fruit of the experience: Darius decrees that everyone should worship the God of Daniel.

Tell-it tips

You will want to prepare this story well before you tell it, varying your tone and speed to build tension and suspense. It involves a repeated phrase with actions. Try it together before you begin. Aim for a very natural, smooth feel to the participation so that it doesn't interrupt the flow of the story. Simply pause and nod at your group when you want them to participate.

Try it together

Everyone says the refrain and does the action together.

Day in *(mime sunrise)*, **day out** *(mime sunset)*

Tell it together

Daniel lived far from home, but he was close to God. **Day in** *(mime sunrise)*, **day out** *(mime sunset)*, three times a day, Daniel knelt by his window to pray. He said 'thank you' and 'sorry' and 'please' when he talked to God, down on his knees.

Daniel was known to be honest and wise, so King Darius often asked for Daniel's advice. **Day in** *(mime sunrise)*, **day out** *(mime sunset)*, they'd chat things through and have a think about what to do.

The king's other advisers grew jealous of this. **Day in** *(mime sunrise)*, **day out** *(mime sunset)*, they began to fizz. They plotted and schemed to get rid of him. **Day in** *(mime sunrise)*, **day out** *(mime sunset)*, they'd make his life grim. They knew that Daniel was a praying man and so devised a nasty plan.

'King, live for ever!' they said. 'Here's what to do. People should pray only to you, **day in** *(mime sunrise)*, **day out** *(mime sunset)*. Yes! Make it a law. Anyone who breaks it should be arrested—and then… thrown into the lions' den!'

'I am the king,' said the king. 'It must be the right thing! **Day in** *(mime sunrise)*, **day out** *(mime sunset)*, from this day on, I declare that everyone will bow to me in prayer. Let the lions who pace about, **day in** *(mime sunrise)*, **day out** *(mime sunset)*, sharpen their claws and close their jaws on anyone who breaks this law.'

Yes. King Darius liked this law a lot. He forgot that Daniel prayed to God—but his other advisers did not.

Day in *(mime sunrise)***, day out** *(mime sunset)*, and especially that day, Daniel got down on his knees to pray. He knew God was greater than any man, so he prayed to God… and then—Daniel was thrown into the lions' den.

Poor King Darius couldn't sleep that night. He ran to the den in the morning light. 'Daniel?' he cried. 'Has your God saved you?'

'King, live for ever!' said Daniel. 'I'm as alive as you. **Day in** *(mime sunrise)***, day out** *(mime sunset)*, God is near. He sent an angel to keep me safe in here.'

'No more claws, jaws and silly laws,' said the king. **Day in** *(mime sunrise)***, day out** *(mime sunset)*, we'll ask God's help with everything.'

19

Esther

Esther saves her people

For your reflection: the book of Esther

Persian King Xerxes divorces his queen and replaces her with a young Jewish woman named Esther. She is an orphan who has been raised by her cousin Mordecai, a palace official. The king does not know they are Jewish. When Mordecai refuses to bow down to Haman, the king's highest in command, Haman conspires to kill every Jew in the empire and persuades the king to agree. Queen Esther must find a way to save her people—Mordecai and herself included.

The story of Esther is dangerous, dramatic and deeply moving. I have tried to capture all those qualities in this retelling.

This story works best with older children, young people and adults.

Tell-it tips

This story, though written in rhyme, is intended as a narrative. Aim to capture the pathos, twists and turns of the story as you tell it. Key words for you to say are in block capitals. The actions for everyone to do together on these key words should flow smoothly as you tell the story. You may like to try it together before you begin.

Try it together

- KING *(mime putting on a crown)*
- QUEEN *(mime putting on a sash)*
- BOW *(take a bow)*

Tell it together

Once there was a KING in Persia who wanted a QUEEN by his side. So he decreed that a search be made far and wide.

Now Esther was a beauty, it couldn't be denied. Her cousin Mordecai loved her like a daughter after her parents died. She was brought to the palace. She was prepared to meet the KING. The KING was very happy and chose Esther to be his QUEEN.

Mordecai worked for the KING at the palace gate, watching those who came in and out every day. He was a loyal servant and a loyal man and often he and Esther thwarted evil plans.

Mordecai served the KING. QUEEN Esther flourished. But the KING didn't know that either one was Jewish.

Now, an official named Haman became the KING's right-hand man. And, as a mark of Haman's power, the KING gave this command— that all of his officials should BOW down low whenever they saw Haman come or go.

Mordecai was mortified, for this he wouldn't do. Mordecai was mortified because he was a Jew—though nobody knew.

Haman was horrified—this wouldn't be allowed. Haman was horrified, because he was sly and cruel and proud. And it was no secret, for everybody knew—Haman hated Jews.

Some of the KING's men went to ask the reason why Mordecai refused to BOW when Haman rode by. The reason for such insolence must surely be uncovered. And that is how Mordecai's secret was discovered.

The next time Mordecai refused to BOW at the palace gate, Haman became so angry that his heart was filled with hate. He wanted rid of every Jew and devised a sneaky plan.

Haman went to the KING and said, 'They disobey your commands. They are not like us at all. Make a royal decree to rid the land of every Jew, and leave the deed to me.'

The decree went out across the land to people everywhere. When Mordecai heard of this, his heart filled with despair. Every single Jew would be killed on a single day—young and old; man, woman and child. No one would get away.

Mordecai was mortified. He got a message to the QUEEN: 'You must go and see the KING and try to stop this wicked thing!'

The QUEEN was horrified. To interfere would be a risk. But Mordecai said, 'You were born for such a time as this!'

The Jewish people prayed while the QUEEN thought what to do. She thought she'd hold a banquet for the KING and invite Haman too.

Haman was proud. Haman was delighted. Haman couldn't help but boast that he had been invited. And yet his anger burned. He called his men around. 'It all means nothing,' he seethed, 'if Mordecai won't BOW down. Tonight, while I enjoy the feast with the KING and QUEEN nearby, you get things ready. For tomorrow Mordecai dies.'

Haman was in for a surprise.

The feast was delicious. The QUEEN truly pleased the KING. 'Ask whatever you will,' he said, 'for I will give you anything.'

Esther cried, 'Please spare my life and save my people too. For Haman has wicked plans to murder every Jew. And Mordecai, who once saved your life, will be murdered too.'

The KING was mortified, for what she said was true.

And so it was that Haman was sentenced there to die. And everything that belonged to him was given to Esther and Mordecai. Mordecai was honoured as the KING's right-hand man and the Jewish people were spared from their enemy's hand.

And to this very day, from the greatest to the least, the Jewish people celebrate and hold a mighty feast.

20

Builder's chant
Jerusalem is rebuilt

For your reflection: the book of Nehemiah

Nehemiah, cupbearer to the king of Persia, steps up to build a team and rebuild the walls and gates of Jerusalem. It takes passion, prayer, faith, courage, planning, hard work and just 52 days to see the job done.

This story-chant captures the teamwork involved and several elements of the building process.

Tell-it tips

This story can be used either before or after Nehemiah's monologue (see below) or can stand on its own. It is light-hearted and loud, and great for large groups. Essentially, it is a set of chants, with a refrain that can be sung. It is patterned on the popular tune 'This is the music concert'. However, it may be most familiar as the song 'If I weren't a girl/ boy scout'. (Search YouTube for guidance.)

The idea is to divide into as many groups as there are verses of the chant (you choose which to include). Everyone sings the chorus together. Each group chants their own verse, adding to the one before as they go along: refrain + 1; refrain + 1 + 2; refrain + 1 + 2 + 3 and so on. Alternatively, each group can keep chanting their own verse while others are added: refrain + 1; refrain + 1/2; refrain + 1/2/3. In either case, the last time, all of the chants are voiced at the same time in a loud, rhythmic cacophony.

Try it together

Start by practising the refrain as a whole group a few times through. Then, divide into as many groups as there are verses. Help each group to practise their verse a few times before you tell the story together.

We're building up our city, there's nothing we'd rather do.
We're building up our city, Nehemiah's building crew,
and as you pass us by, you will hear us cry…

Tell it together

Refrain

We're building up our city, there's nothing we'd rather do.
We're building up our city, Nehemiah's building crew,
and as you pass us by, you will hear us cry…

1. Nehemiah
   He's our man
   He has got the building plan

2. 2, 4, 6, 8
   Raise the walls *(mime walls)*
   Fix the gates *(open gate)*

3. Grab a weapon
   Watch your back *(search with right hand over eyes)*
   Ready for attack *(search with left hand over eyes)*

4. Every hour *(look at watch)*
   Stand on guard *(stand straight and click heels)*
   In the power of the Lord *(point to heaven)*

5.   Zip, zip, zip *(as if sawing)*
     Ooo, I threw my hip *(hand on hip as if sore)*
     Crunch (clap once)

6   Two by four *(gesture plank of wood)*
     Nail it to the floor *(as if hammering)*
     Ouch *(shake thumb as if struck by hammer)*

7.   Time for coffee *(sip coffee)*
     Time for tea *(sip tea)*
     Ooooh, I need a wee *(cross legs)*

8.   Stir the mortar till it sticks *(stirring)*
     Build it, build it *(fist on fist)*
     Quick, quick, quick *(punch the air three times)*

9.   Push it up *(push something heavy)*
     Pull it up *(hoist a bucket on rope)*
     Look out below *(Look down)*
     Crash (clap)

10   On the double *(run on the spot)*
     Pick up rubble *(pretend to pick up heavy rocks)*
     Go! Go! Go! *(punch the air three times)*

11. Day and night *(sway arms above head to the left)*
     Night and day *(sway arms above head to the right)*
     Lift your voice in praise *(arms up worshipfully)*

12   Amen, Amen *(hands in prayer, palms together)*
     The walls are built again *(building movement, fist on fist)*
     Yes (punch the air)

21

Nehemiah's monologue
The temple walls and gates are rebuilt

For your reflection: The book of Nehemiah

The exiles who are returning to Jerusalem are living in the rubbled remains of the city, defenceless and disgraced. Nehemiah, who works in the palace in Persia, despairs. Though he seems an unlikely leader, he is granted a leave of absence to oversee the rebuilding of the city walls and gates. Despite opposition and seemingly insurmountable odds, Nehemiah and his workforce complete the task in quick time. Ezra, the priest, reads God's law and the people confess and pledge themselves to God.

This story works best with older children, young people and adults.

Tell-it tips

This is a mini monologue. It is told from Nehemiah's point of view and is sober and determined in tone. It is written in rhyme, but this should be subtle and understated.

Try it together

You may want to try the 'Builder's chant' (see Chapter 20) together as a story starter.

Tell it together

It was my brother who told me what they had seen—the city gates burned, the walls in a heap. It broke my heart, made me churn, kept me from my sleep.

So I prayed to the Lord in my distress. I prayed and I said, 'I do confess that we as a people have been in a heap, exiled these years for our failure to keep your law and your ways. But to hear of our city is the saddest of days. Those who have returned to Jerusalem are disgraced and in trouble, defences laid waste in a pile of rubble. Remember those who honour you alone. Remember your promise to bring us back home.'

I worked for the king then, in that foreign land—a king who was also a king of a man. He saw I was troubled and bid me to go, not to wait—to rebuild our people, the walls and the gates. He gave me his help in all that I asked, safe passage and timber to help with our task.

It would take careful planning for us to succeed. It would take every effort to achieve every deed. It would take a great team built from those who'd been scattered, disheartened, downtrodden, hopes daily shattered. And while the walls of the city would rise from the ground, the walls of apathy and resentment would need knocking down. There would be enemies from inside and out to oppose and frustrate, create hate and doubt.

But God gave the vision and I was the one to lead in God's power and get the work done. With singular purpose we began our repairs—put faith into action, feet to our prayers. The work was heavy, hot and hard, but we worked in the joy and the strength of the Lord. Despite opposition and fear of attack, God had our devotion and God had our back.

The walls of the city rose from the ground, the gates were established and all those around were astonished when the walls of Jerusalem were strong once again. It didn't take long—just 52 days. The law of Moses was read aloud and the city was filled with God's praise.

New Testament stories

22

The angel said, 'Don't worry'

Advent angel stories

For your reflection: Matthew 1:18–25; Luke 1:26–38; John 6:20

Angels are everywhere in the Advent stories—informing, encouraging, guiding, protecting and, of course, worshipping. They appear in the lives of ordinary people, revealing that the living God is entering their everyday world.

This retelling captures the joy of their message, 'God is bringing you good news.'

Tell-it tips

This story combines the angel stories of Advent. It has a funky, feel-good rhythm. You will need to prepare well to tell well. There is a spoken refrain with actions. There is also a call-and-response element, in which you will say a phrase and your group will respond with the appropriate gesture.

Try it together

First, practise this refrain with actions a few times together before you begin.

The angel said *(flap arms, palms down)*,
'Don't worry' *(turn palms, elbows bent, shake head)*.
The angel said *(flap arms, palms down)*,
'Don't worry' *(turn palms, elbows bent, shake head)*.
The angel said *(flap arms, palms down)*,
'Don't worry' *(turn palms, elbows bent, shake head)*.
'I'm bringing you good news' *(palms up, arms out in front of you)*.

The last time, the refrain changes to:

Jesus said, 'Don't worry… *(palms up, elbows bent, shake head)*.
I'm bringing you good news' *(arms out as if giving a gift)*.

Then explain that you will say each of the following phrases yourself and everyone will do the actions. Try it together.

- Mary found it scary **(scary face)**.
- Joseph got the jitters **(knock knees nervously)**.
- Bethlehem got busy **(bump the person next to you)**.
- The shepherds got the shivers **(shocked shivers)**.
- Jesus is the Saviour **(mime rocking a baby)**.

Tell it together

Mary found it scary *(scary face)*.
Mary found it scary *(scary face)*.
Mary found it scary *(scary face)*
when the angel first appeared.

The angel said *(flap arms, palms down)*,
'Don't worry' *(turn palms, elbows bent, shake head)*.
The angel said *(flap arms, palms down)*,
'Don't worry' *(turn palms, elbows bent, shake head)*.

The angel said *(flap arms, palms down)*,
'Don't worry' *(turn palms, elbows bent, shake head)*.
'I'm bringing you good news' *(palms up, arms out in front of you)*.

'A babe is born to you.
I'm bringing you good news.'

Joseph got the jitters *(knock knees nervously)*.
Joseph got the jitters *(knock knees nervously)*.
Joseph got the jitters *(knock knees nervously)*.
When the angel first appeared.

The angel said *(flap arms, palms down)*,
'Don't worry' *(turn palms, elbows bent, shake head)*.
The angel said *(flap arms, palms down)*,
'Don't worry' *(turn palms, elbows bent, shake head)*.
The angel said *(flap arms, palms down)*,
'Don't worry' *(turn palms, elbows bent, shake head)*.
'I'm bringing you good news' *(palms up, arms out in front of you)*.

'No need to sing the blues.
I'm bringing you good news.'

Bethlehem got busy *(bump the person next to you)*.
Bethlehem got busy *(bump the person next to you)*.
Bethlehem got busy *(bump the person next to you)*.
When the angels first appeared.

The angel said *(flap arms, palms down)*,
'Don't worry' *(turn palms, elbows bent, shake head)*.
The angel said *(flap arms, palms down)*,
'Don't worry' *(turn palms, elbows bent, shake head)*.
The angel said *(flap arms, palms down)*,
'Don't worry' *(turn palms, elbows bent, shake head)*.
'I'm bringing you good news' *(palms up, arms out in front of you)*.

'Peace on earth. Good will to all!
We're bringing you good news.'

The shepherds got the shivers *(shocked shivers)*.
The shepherds got the shivers *(shocked shivers)*.
The shepherds got the shivers *(shocked shivers)*.
When the angels first appeared.

The angel said *(flap arms, palms down)*,
'Don't worry' *(turn palms, elbows bent, shake head)*.
The angel said *(flap arms, palms down)*,
'Don't worry' *(turn palms, elbows bent, shake head)*.
The angel said *(flap arms, palms down)*,
'Don't worry' *(turn palms, elbows bent, shake head)*.
'I'm bringing you good news' *(palms up, arms out in front of you)*.

'Put on your running shoes.
We're bringing you good news.'

Jesus is the Saviour *(mime rocking a baby)*.
Jesus is the Saviour *(mime rocking a baby)*.
Jesus is the Saviour *(mime rocking a baby)*
who was born so long ago.

Jesus said, 'Don't worry' *(turn palms, elbows bent, shake head)*.
Jesus said, 'Don't worry' *(turn palms, elbows bent, shake head)*.
Jesus said, 'Don't worry' *(turn palms, elbows bent, shake head)*.
'I'm bringing you good news!' *(palms up and out in front of you as if giving a gift)*.

God is with us. Jesus saves!
I'm bringing you good news!

23

People here, people there
Jesus is born

For your reflection: Matthew 1; Luke 2:1–20

Joseph and Mary are both visited by angels delivering the good news that they will have God's Son—the Saviour of the world. While Mary is heavily pregnant, they must travel to Bethlehem to be counted in a census. The town is packed with people and there is nowhere for them to stay except a stable offered to them by one of the innkeepers. It is there that Jesus is born—to save 'people here, people there, all kinds of people everywhere!'

This retelling captures the inclusive nature of God's salvation for us all, as well as the busy bustle of Bethlehem.

Tell-it tips

This is an active participation story which involves people changing places with one another. If you are in a tight space or there is not enough room to swap places, simply turn around on the spot instead. You will want to try it together before you start.

Try it together

The following refrain appears in the story. Explain that you will say the key words and everyone will do the action. Try it together.

People here *(high five or shake hands with the person on your right)*, people there *(high five or shake hands with the person on your left)*, all kinds of people everywhere *(change places with the person next to you, or, if there is space, someone from across the room)*.

Tell it together

Mary was more than a little surprised when an angel suddenly appeared to see her.

'Don't be afraid,' said the angel. 'God has chosen you! There is nothing that God can't do. You will be the mother of God's own Son. He will show people how to live for God and he will forgive them the wrong they've done.'

People here *(high five or shake hands with the person on your right)*, people there *(high five or shake hands with the person on your left)*, all kinds of people everywhere *(change places with the person next to you, or, if there is space, someone from across the room)*.

Joseph was more than a little surprised when an angel suddenly appeared to see him.

'Don't be afraid,' said the angel. 'God has chosen you too! You will be a husband to Mary and an earthly father to God's own Son. He will show people how to live for God and he will forgive them the wrong they've done.'

People here *(high five or shake hands with the person on your right)*, people there *(high five or shake hands with the person on your left)*, all kinds of people everywhere *(change places with the person next to you, or, if there is space, someone from across the room)*.

When it was almost time for the baby to be born, Mary and Joseph travelled to Bethlehem. They tried to find a place to stay, but all of the inns were full that day.

People here *(high five or shake hands with the person on your right)*, people there *(high five or shake hands with the person on your left)*, all kinds of people everywhere *(change places with the person next to you, or, if there is space, someone from across the room)*.

An innkeeper said, 'You can stay in my barn.' So Mary and Joseph did their best to settle down and have a rest. It wasn't long until the time had come! Mary had a baby Son. They named him Jesus. It means 'God saves'.

People here *(high five or shake hands with the person on your right)*, people there *(high five or shake hands with the person on your left)*, all kinds of people everywhere *(change places with the person next to you, or, if there is space, someone from across the room)*.

24

Long, long ago on a dark, dark night
wise men visit Jesus

For your reflection: Matthew 2:1–12

Stargazing wise men from the east spot an unusual new star, a sign that a new king has been born. They follow the star. Along the way, they arrive in Jerusalem and ask King Herod if he knows where the child is. Herod discovers that the Messiah is to be born in Bethlehem. He sends them there and asks them to report back, once they find the child.

The wise men find and worship Jesus, giving him gifts. They are warned in a dream not to return to Herod and they go home another way. In a bid to protect the throne and his position, King Herod orders the killing of all boys up to the age of two. Joseph and Mary take Jesus and flee to safety in Egypt.

This retelling is a travel tale. Enjoy the journey.

Tell-it tips

This story has strong rhythm and rhyme. Remember to create pace and mood and tension. Practise saying the refrain together a few times and repeat it together throughout the story. The phrase 'in the early light' in the last sentence will come as an unanticipated surprise. Your audience will naturally join in during the first part of the refrain—but pause, whisper 'shhhh', gesture for quiet and say the words 'in the early light' by yourself.

Note: The more familiar you are with the story before you tell it, the more effective and enjoyable the experience will be for everyone.

Try it together

Invite everyone to say this refrain together. Explain that you will gesture to them to say it with you as you tell the story.

Long, long ago on a dark, dark night.

Tell it together

Long, long ago on a dark, dark night,
some very wise men saw a very bright light.
A big new star in the big dark sky,
a big new question, 'Why, oh why,
was the star so bright?'
Long, long ago on a dark, dark night.

Long, long ago on a dark, dark night
the wise men said, 'What a sight!
What does it mean, this amazing thing?
A brand new star for a brand new king!'
That's why it burned so bright,
long, long ago on a dark, dark night.

Long, long ago on a dark, dark night
the wise men said, 'Let's follow the light
and find the babe, the newborn king,
and give to him the gifts we'll bring.'
They set their course on the star so bright,
long, long ago on a dark, dark night.

Long, long ago on a dark, dark night
the wise men found King Herod the great.
'Where can we find the newborn king?
We have come to worship him.
We saw his star burn so bright
long, long ago on a dark, dark night.'

Long, long ago on a dark, dark night
the wise men thought King Herod polite.
'Find the child and tell me too
so I can worship him just like you.'
But dark, dark plans were born of spite
long, long ago on a dark, dark night.

Long, long ago on a dark, dark night
the wise men said, 'Let's follow the light.'
And so they left Jerusalem
in search of the babe in Bethlehem
'We're here!' they said with such delight,
Long, long ago on a dark, dark night.

Long, long ago on a dark, dark night
they bowed to the boy with a smile so bright
and gave him gold fit for a king,
incense and myrrh—for suffering.
But how could they know—
long, long ago on a dark, dark night?

Long, long ago on a dark, dark night
wise men were warned in a dream so bright.
'Do not go home through Jerusalem!'
So they took another route from Bethlehem,
and wondered on their wanders in the starry night
long, long ago *(pause and whisper 'shhhhh')* **in the early light.**

25

Down by the river
Jesus is baptised

For your reflection: Matthew 3:13–17; Mark 1:9–11;
Luke 3:1–22; John 1:29–34

John the Baptist preaches repentance and baptises people as a symbol of cleansing. When Jesus (now aged around 30) comes to be baptised, John is reluctant. His hesitancy comes from a place of deep humility: Jesus has never done anything for which he needs to repent. Jesus is baptised anyway, as an example of humble obedience to God. The heavens open, the Spirit of God comes down as a dove and God's voice is heard to say, 'This is my Son, whom I love; with him I am well pleased.'

Tell-it tips

This is a gently rhythmic story with a thoughtful tone. It has a strong lilting feel to reflect the lapping of water and the steady flow of people coming to be baptised.

Try it together

These three refrains appear in the story. Explain that you will say each one yourself as you come to it in the story, then you will gesture to everyone to repeat it with you. Try it together.

So people came down to the river, down to the river they came.
People came down to the river to show that they wanted
    to change.

Jesus came into the river, into the river he came.
Jesus came into the river and John was quite amazed!

So Jesus went under the water, and out of the water he came.
Jesus went under the water to show he would live God's way.

Tell it together

John was preaching loud and clear. 'God's promised one will soon
    be here!
Love God! Live God's way! Come and be baptised today!'

So people came down to the river, down to the river they came.
People came down to the river to show that they wanted to change!
So people came down to the river, down to the river they came.
People came down to the river to show that they wanted
    to change.

Into the river people came—fathers, mothers, sons and daughters.
Into the river people came to be baptised in its waters.

Jesus came into the river, into the river he came.
Jesus came into the river and John was quite amazed!
Jesus came into the river, into the river he came.
Jesus came into the river and John was quite amazed!

'Why have you come to be baptised? You are God's promised one.
I should be baptised by you! You've never done anything wrong.
'I've come to do what God wants, John, so let God's will be done.
I've come to do what God wants, so let God's will be done.'

So Jesus went under the water and out of the water he came.
Jesus went under the water to show he would live God's way.
So Jesus went under the water, and out of the water he came.
Jesus went under the water to show he would live God's way.

A voice came from the heavens, 'This is my Son, the one that I love!'
And down came the Spirit of God, the Spirit of God came down like
a dove.

26

Get your nets
Jesus calls his followers

For your reflection: Matthew 4:18–22; Mark 1:16–30;
Luke 5:1–11

Before Jesus begins his ministry, he faces gruelling spiritual opposition in the desert. Satan tempts him to abandon his identity and mission, but Jesus proves himself and resists. When he emerges from the desert, Jesus begins to gather a group of twelve unlikely disciples around him. Over the next three years, they will be fully immersed in his life and ministry, learning all that they can from him. They will listen to his stories, witness his compassion, be astonished by his miracles and experience first-hand the close relationship he has with the Father.

In this retelling, Jesus calls Peter, Andrew, James and John to leave their fishing nets and join him.

Tell-it tips

This story includes a verse sung to the tune of 'Row, row, row your boat'. Try it together, with actions, until everyone gets the hang of it. Then, when the time comes, you can play with it—speeding it up or slowing it down. You may ask people to pair up, hold hands and sing while rowing. You may even want to divide your group in half and have each side sing the verse to the other, sing it in a round or sing it while rowing forward and back toward each other. It has been adapted from *100s of Songs, Games and More* (Cook Communications, 2003).

Try it together

Sing the verse together, with actions.

Get, get, get your net *(gather your net)*,
throw it in the sea *(toss your net)*.
Pull it in all full of fish *(pull in your heavy net)*,
then come and follow me *(walk on the spot)*.

There is also a tongue-twister opportunity, should you wish to make use of it during the telling. Try it together a few times together as a whole group. Then choose a volunteer to join you and, every time you come to the tongue-twister in the text, encourage the volunteer to say it.

More fish than a fisherman could wish for.

Note: It is well worth revisiting 'Prepare well' and 'Tell well' on pages 14–27 as you prepare this story.

Tell it together

By the time morning came, Peter, Andrew, James and John had been fishing all night. They had been hoping for **more fish than a fisherman could wish for**, but they hadn't caught a thing. Now they were washing their nets.

There was a crowd on the beach, listening to Jesus teach. 'Everyone can be part of God's kingdom,' he said.

The crowd got bigger and bigger and the space for Jesus got smaller and smaller. So Jesus got into Peter's boat and they bobbed away from shore. Even then, Jesus kept on teaching.

When Jesus was finished, he turned to Peter and said:

Get, get, get your net *(gather your net)*,
throw it in the sea *(toss your net)*.
Pull it in all full of fish *(pull in your heavy net)*,
then come and follow me *(walk on the spot)*.

Peter was not convinced. 'We've been fishing all night and not got a nibble.'

But Jesus said:

Get, get, get your net *(gather your net)*,
throw it in the sea *(toss your net)*.
Pull it in all full of fish *(pull in your heavy net)*,
then come and follow me *(walk on the spot)*.

'OK,' said Peter, as he threw the nets into the sea.

Suddenly, there were **more fish than a fisherman could wish for**! The nets were bursting.

'Come and help!' shouted Peter to the others. Soon both boats were so full they began to sink.

'Come on,' Jesus said to them. 'Follow me and we'll fish for people until God's kingdom is bursting.'

Get, get, get your net *(gather your net)*,
throw it in the sea *(toss your net)*.
Pull it in all full of fish *(pull in your heavy net)*,
then come and follow me *(walk on the spot)*.

27

A few good friends
The man on the mat

For your reflection: Matthew 9:1–8; Mark 2:3–12; Luke 5:18–25

The miracles and teachings of Jesus attract swarms of people. One day, a man who is paralysed is brought by four friends to Jesus for healing. They can get nowhere near Jesus, so they knock a hole through the roof of the house where he is teaching and lower their friend down to Jesus. Jesus delights in their show of faith, heals the man and forgives his sin too. The Jewish scholars instantly object, saying that only God can forgive sins. Jesus makes it clear that he has the power to do both.

This retelling captures the joy of friendship, the strength of faith, the compassion of Jesus and the delight of new beginnings.

Tell-it tips

This is a fun call-and-response story with actions. Simply ask your group to clap their hands once on every word that rhymes with 'mat' (written in block capitals throughout) and give a high five to the person next to them every time you say the word 'friends'.

If you have time, you may want to tell the story a second time and quicken the pace.

Tell it together

There was once a man on a MAT. The man on the MAT just SAT. He couldn't stand or walk or crawl. In fact, he couldn't move at all, and THAT might have been the end of THAT…

But four good FRIENDS came around.

They said, 'Jesus is here in our town! He's giving a talk! He can help you to walk!' And they lifted the MAT off the ground.

The man had a happy ride with all of his FRIENDS at his side. But his heart soon filled with gloom. 'Look! There's no room! How will we ever get inside?'

His FRIENDS had a little CHAT. Then they carried the man on his MAT. They climbed on to the roof that was FLAT. They made it their goal to dig a big hole and lower him to where Jesus was AT.

Jesus looked at the man, amazed. Then he looked up at each FRIEND's face. He saw faith in their eyes, of a very large size, and said, 'You've come to just the right place.

All is forgiven and well. Rise from where you are AT!'

The man got up and carried his MAT. He jumped, and skipped and walked by himself—and THAT was the beginning of THAT!

28

How not to worry

Jesus teaches about trust

For your reflection: Matthew 6:19–21, 25–34; Matthew 7:7–12

The Sermon on the Mount captures the essence of Jesus' teaching. It is famous for the Beatitudes—Jesus' teaching that God's kingdom is not full of the rich and mighty, but of those who are poor in spirit. There are also broad principles about how we should treat each other—the need for commitment and forgiveness. This retelling focuses on the need to trust God for everything.

Tell-it tips

This story captures the setting (a lovely day on the hillside) and uses a song to affirm the point of the story—which is to be thankful and trust God when we are worried.

Try it together

Sing this adapted version of the round 'I love the flowers' (popularly known as the 'Boom-de-ah-da song') before you tell the story and again afterwards. Sing it all together a few times before breaking it into a two- or four-part round. (Note: If you don't know the melody, it can be found on page 11 of *The Round Book* by Margaret Read MacDonald and Winifred Jaeger.)

1. Thanks for the flowers *(pick flower)*, thanks for the birds that fly *(flap wings)*.
2. Thanks for the sunshine *(make sun with arms)*, thanks for the starry sky *(splash stars in the sky)*.
3. Thanks for your love and care *(hands on heart)* and our daily bread *(hands out to receive)*.
4. Thanks-be-to-you, thanks-be-to-you, thanks-be-to-you, thanks.

Last time: Thanks-be-to-you, thanks-be-to-you, thanks-be-to-you, thanks, amen.

Tell it together

1. Thanks for the flowers *(pick flower)*, thanks for the birds that fly *(flap wings)*.
2. Thanks for the sunshine *(make sun with arms)*, thanks for the starry sky *(splash stars in the sky)*.
3. Thanks for your love and care *(hands on heart)* and our daily bread *(hands out to receive)*.
4. Thanks-be-to-you, thanks-be-to-you, thanks-be-to-you, thanks.

Last time: Thanks-be-to-you, thanks-be-to-you, thanks-be-to-you, thanks, amen.

Jesus was teaching on a hillside. It was a lovely day. The birds were singing. The flowers were blooming. But people were worrying, as people often do.

'Don't worry about what you will eat or drink or wear,' said Jesus. 'Just look at the birds in the air. They don't sow seeds for food to eat. God takes care of all their needs. Will worrying make you stronger or help you live longer?

'See the flowers that grow? They don't sew clothes so they will look good. God makes them beautiful. God is good.

'God loves you even more than the birds and the flowers. There's more to life than fashion and food. God will take care of you. God is good.

'If you look for something, you will find it. If you knock on a door, someone answers it. If you ask your parents for bread, do they give you a stone instead? Ask God for what you need and you will receive it. God is good. Do you believe it?

'Don't put your trust in the things that you own. Things are easily lost or stolen or worn. Trust in God. You'll have treasure in heaven. Thank God for all the good you are given.

'Worry doesn't change a thing. Trust God for everything.'

1. Thanks for the flowers *(pick flower)*, thanks for the birds that fly *(flap wings)*.
2. Thanks for the sunshine *(make sun with arms)*, thanks for the starry sky *(splash stars in the sky)*.
3. Thanks for your love and care *(hands on heart)* and our daily bread *(hands out to receive)*.
4. Thanks-be-to-you, thanks-be-to-you, thanks-be-to-you, thanks.

Last time: Thanks-be-to-you, thanks-be-to-you, thanks-be-to-you, thanks, amen.

29

Hushabye lake

Jesus calms the storm

For your reflection: Mark 4:35–41; Luke 8:22–25

One evening, Jesus and his disciples are travelling by boat. Jesus is exhausted. He falls asleep so soundly that not even a sudden and fierce storm wakes him. The disciples, many of whom are experienced fishermen, are terrified. They wake Jesus. He stretches out his hand and commands the storm to stop. This remarkable story displays both Jesus' humanity and his divinity.

Tell-it tips

This story has a meditative lullaby feel, except during the tension of the storm. It works very well as a blessing. The participation element of this story takes place before the story is told and should leave everyone feeling relaxed and ready to listen. Essentially, you will be mimicking the movements and sound of rolling waves.

Try it together

Invite your group to stand; posture should be relaxed and soft. Repeat each of the following gestures or actions as feels right. Ask the group to do what you are doing.

- Roll your head to the right.
- Roll your head to the left.

- Put your arms out to your side with your palms open and roll your wrists forward in gentle waves; then add gentle arm rolls.
- Keep your arms out to your side and sweep them forward and back in a gentle wave motion; lean your body into this motion.
- Reverse the above actions.
- Ask everyone to sit down.

Tell it together

Jesus was weary. It had been a long day. He said to his helpers, 'Let's sail away, away, away; let's get in a boat and sail away.'

So they found a boat bobbing by the shushabye shore and sailed out a little way, then sailed out some more.

The waves gently lapped on the lullaby lake. The wind whispered low and Jesus soon fell asleep in the hushabye boat, hushabye, hushabye, hushabye boat.

Then suddenly the lake kicked up such a fuss! Thunder boomed, lightning flashed and winds rushabye rushed. Rain lashed; waves grew strong; the boat tossed about. Jesus' helpers began to shout! 'Wake up, Jesus! We are going to drown! How can you sleep so sound?'

Jesus stood up and stretched out his hand.

'Hushabye, hushabye,' he said to the waves.

'Hushabye, hushabye,' he said to the wind.

'Hushabye, hushabye,' he said to his friends. 'Don't be afraid. I am near. You can be brave.'

The waves gently lapped on the lullaby lake. Jesus' helpers whispered low. How did Jesus shush the storm? Then they all sailed away in the hushabye boat; they all sailed away, away to the shushabye shore.

30

A shared lunch

Jesus feeds 5000

For your reflection: Matthew 14:15–21; Mark 6:35–44;
Luke 9:12–17; John 6:1–13

Jesus and his disciples spend a long day ministering to a crowd of over 5000 people. Everyone is hungry but there is no food. The disciples suggest that Jesus should send everyone home. Instead, Jesus suggests that they should feed the crowd. A boy in the crowd offers his lunch and Jesus miraculously turns it into a feast that feeds everyone, with lots left over.

The next day, many in the same crowd seek him out again. He accuses them of coming back for miracles and physical bread when what they should be seeking is the spiritual bread from heaven. 'I am the bread that gives life,' he says. 'Everyone who eats it will live for ever' (see John 6:35).

Tell-it tips

This story has a lilting rhythm and joyous tone. It includes a single refrain with actions, repeated several times throughout. You will want to try it together before you begin. Pause and gesture for participation as the refrain arises in the story.

Try it together

Practise the refrain and actions together.

Two fish *(wiggle hand like a swimming fish)*
and five bits of bread *(lay your left hand flat out in front of you, palm up; slide your right hand over your left palm as if slicing bread).*

Tell it together

'Let's go and see Jesus!' a little boy said. So his mum packed some lunch: **two fish** *(wiggle hand)* **and five bits of bread** *(slicing action).*
Off they went with a skip and a song to spend time with Jesus all that day long.

Five thousand others had gathered there too, to listen to Jesus and see what he'd do.
He healed those who were sick or blind or lame, and talked about God's love until sunset came.

Everyone was hungry, but no one would leave, so Jesus said to his helpers, 'Give them something to eat.'
'We've no food or money,' said Philip, 'so there's no way we can! You must send them all home. That's the best plan.'

But Jesus smiled to himself and said out loud, 'See what you can find, out in the crowd.'
Just then the little boy tugged on Andrew and said, 'Here are **two fish** *(wiggle hand)* **and five bits of bread** *(slicing action).*'

'Just **two fish** *(wiggle hand)* **and five bits of bread** *(slicing action)* will not feed this crowd,' Andrew said.

'Time for a picnic,' Jesus said with a smile. 'Tell everyone to sit for a while.'
He took the **two fish** *(wiggle hand)* **and five bits of bread** *(slicing action)*, broke the bread and bowed his head.

He lifted his voice to God in prayer: 'Thank you for your daily care.'
Then to everyone's surprise, everyone was fed from just **two fish** *(wiggle hand)* **and five bits of bread** *(slicing action)*.

There were even twelve baskets of food to spare from the **two fish** *(wiggle hand)* **and five bits of bread** *(slicing action)* the little boy shared.

When they went to see Jesus the next day, he said, 'People need me. I am the bread.'

31

The busy sister

Mary listens to Jesus

For your reflection: Luke 10:38–42

Jesus and his disciples stop at the house of Martha in Bethany. She shares her home with her sister Mary and their brother Lazarus, whom Jesus raised from the dead. Mary sits at Jesus' feet and listens to everything he has to say. Martha, meanwhile, is distracted with preparing and serving the meal for everyone. She becomes frustrated and asks Jesus whether he cares that Mary has left her to fix the meal alone. She asks Jesus to tell Mary to help.

Luke's Gospel tells us: 'Martha, Martha,' the Lord answered, 'you are worried and upset about many things, but few things are needed—or indeed only one. Mary has chosen what is better, and it will not be taken away from her.'

Tell-it tips

This story works well in a variety of ways and simply involves your group in repeating actions after you during the story. You can tell it together as a whole group with everyone repeating the same gestures together, or you can divide the group into two smaller groups—'Marthas' and 'Marys'.

Actions for your group to do after you appear in bold in the story below. They will be picked up naturally as you go along, provided that you do the action first and gesture to your group to repeat it with you. 'Martha' gestures should be overdramatised with lots of impatience and huffing and puffing as you go along. 'Mary' gestures should be calm.

Try it together

Invite everyone to do the actions with you as you go along.

Tell it together

Martha and Mary were happy when Jesus and his friends came to visit them. While Martha got busy making a feast, Mary sat and listened at Jesus' feet.

Martha scrubbed *(scrubbing)*, peeled *(peeling)*, diced and sliced *(dicing and slicing)*.

Mary listened to Jesus *(hand to ear, smiling)*.

Martha measured *(measuring)*, mixed *(mixing)*, kneaded and baked *(kneading and baking)*.

Mary listened to Jesus *(other hand to ear, nodding)*.

Martha set the table *(setting the table)* and poured the wine *(pouring the wine)*.

Mary listened to Jesus *(both hands to ears, smiling and nodding)*.

'It's not fair,' Martha puffed.
'I'm doing all the work,' Martha whined.
'I've had enough!' Martha huffed.

'I'm being busy!' she said to Jesus. 'Mary is being lazy! Will you ask her to help me?'

'Dear Martha, can't you see?' Jesus smiled. 'Mary is spending time with me. While you are busy being stressed, Mary has chosen what is best.'

When we spend time with Jesus, we are blessed *(gesture to everyone to put both hands to ears and listen)*.

32

A well man thanks Jesus

The ten men healed of leprosy

For your reflection: Luke 17: 11–19

On his way to Jerusalem, Jesus travels along the border between Samaria and Galilee. As he is going into a village, ten men who have leprosy meet him, calling out to him for pity from a distance because they can't go near. When he sees them, he feels compassion. He tells them to go and show themselves to the priests, and as they go, they are healed. One of them comes back, praising God. He throws himself at Jesus' feet and thanks him. He is a Samaritan. Jesus praises him for his thankfulness and his faith.

Tell-it tips

This story is a mini monologue and is reflective in tone. It includes a simple refrain to say together before and after the story. You will want try it together a few times until it is smooth.

Try it together

We run and jump and praise the Lord *(run and jump on the spot with arms up)*,
say thank you to the Lord.
We kneel down low and bow our heads *(bow heads, hands in prayer)*,
say thank you to the Lord.

Tell it together

We were untouchable. That's what people called us. That's what we were. Our skin was raw; our fingers were numb. Our clothes had become as ragged as our bodies. We covered our faces and shouted, 'Unclean! Unclean!' so that no one would come near. And no one did. We were even untouchable to God—or so it seemed.

We were huddled together outside the city when we saw Jesus coming. 'Help us, Jesus! Please heal us!' we shouted from our distance. It was unthinkable, but Jesus came close.

When I looked into his eyes I saw my own suffering there. 'Go and let the priest look at you,' he said to us gently. 'He will see that you are well.'

By the time we turned to go, we were completely healed. We were so excited! We could go back to our families and our lives. The others ran ahead—but I ran back, praising God. Then I knelt down in front of Jesus and thanked him over and over again.

'There were ten of you,' he said, 'but you are the only one who came back to thank God. You can go home now. Your faith has made you well.'

We run and jump and praise the Lord *(run and jump on the spot with arms up)*,
say thank you to the Lord.
We kneel down low and bow our heads *(bow heads, hands in prayer)*,
say thank you to the Lord.

33

A big change
Zacchaeus meets Jesus

For your reflection: Luke 19:1–10

The Jewish leaders are not happy about the known 'sinners' that Jesus spends time with. Zacchaeus is a case in point. Here we have a conniving tax collector who not only works for the Romans but overtaxes his own people, the Jews, and pockets the profit for himself.

When Jesus comes to town, Zacchaeus is as excited as anyone else. By the time Jesus leaves town again, Zacchaeus is a changed man. He offers to give half of his money to the poor and repays what he has cheated from everyone else in abundance.

This retelling captures the essence of what Jesus has come to do—transform lives.

Tell-it tips

This is a response story. You will tell the story and everyone will do the actions together. You may want to try it together before you begin. Equally, you could just tell the story and let the participation arise naturally.

Try it together

Shut the curtains *(shut curtains)*
Tried to hide *(peek out)*

A little here *(right hand out)*
A little there *(left hand out)*

Curtains opened *(open curtains)*
Doors swung wide *(open door with a creak)*

Couldn't see over *(tiptoes gesture, peering over)*
Couldn't see through *(bend down low)*

Climbed up *(climbing up)*
Climbed down *(climbing down)*

Tell it together

Zacchaeus wasn't very tall. Zacchaeus wasn't liked at all. He
cheated folks and often lied. So they shut the curtains *(shut
curtains)* and tried to hide *(peek out)* when they saw him coming
round to get the taxes in their town.

He kept some of the money for himself, it's true, the way that
cheaters often do—a little here *(right hand out)*, a little there *(left
hand out)*. Zacchaeus didn't care that he wasn't liked at all, though
sometimes he wished he wasn't so small.

Like the day he heard someone say, 'Look! It's Jesus! And he's
coming our way!'

Curtains opened *(open curtains)*, doors swung wide *(open door
with a creak)*—everyone from everywhere gathered outside.

They wanted to see Jesus. Zacchaeus wanted to see him too. But no matter how hard he tried, he couldn't see over *(tiptoes gesture, peering over)* and he couldn't see through *(bend down low)*. He was just too small.

'I can't see Jesus at all,' said Zacchaeus.

That's when he remembered with joy the tree he climbed up *(climbing up)* and climbed down *(climbing down)* as a boy.

And that's how he gleefully came to be happily perched in a sycamore tree.

'I can see Jesus,' said Zacchaeus. 'What a great view!'

And that is how Jesus got a good view too.

'Come down, Zacchaeus,' Jesus said. 'I'd like to spend some time with you!'

So from the tree he'd climbed up *(climbing up)*, he climbed down *(climbing down)* and walked with Jesus back through the town— back through the crowd he couldn't see over *(tiptoes gesture, peering over)* or through *(bend down low)* to his own house, where the curtains were opened *(open curtains)* and the door swung out wide *(open door with a creak)*. Zacchaeus invited Jesus inside.

Now those who didn't like Zacchaeus at all were very unhappy by what they saw.

'How can Jesus go to his house to eat? Doesn't he know that Zacchaeus is a liar and cheat?'

That may be as was, but was no more by the time Zacchaeus came back out his front door.

'I will give half of all I have to those who are poor, and pay everyone back four times more!' he said.

And that is what he did.

A little here *(right hand out)*, a little there *(left hand out)*—the people of the town began to welcome Zacchaeus when he came around. Zacchaeus cared for one and all. He was also quite glad that he was small.

Like on the day he heard Jesus say, 'Zacchaeus! You have been saved today!'

34

The one who loves

Jesus promises to send the Holy Spirit

For your reflection: John 14:15–21

In this brief but powerful passage, Jesus reminds us again of love. He also promises to send the Holy Spirit, the very one who will help us to practise toward others the love we profess to have for Jesus. He also emphasises the unity between Father, Son and Holy Spirit.

The promise of the Holy Spirit comes to fruition during Pentecost (Acts 2:1–31). The disciples return to Jerusalem to wait, just as Jesus has instructed them. Ten days after his ascension, the Holy Spirit arrives, flooding the room with the sound of wind. Above each person's head is a hovering flame. They speak in languages that are not their own but are understood. They are given power to convince many people of their message.

But for now, the promise.

Tell-it tips

This is a very simple, reflective and effective rhyme.

Try it together

Say the words in bold together, as an echo. If you prefer, you can divide a large group into two smaller groups (see below). You will want to try this together a few times as a group before you begin.

You say:
If you say you love me,
you must do what I told you to—
show your love for others
in what you say and do.

Whole group echoes:
If we say we love you
we must do what you tell us to—
show our love for others
in what we say and do.

Or group 1 echoes:
If we say we love you
we must do what you tell us to—

And group 2 echoes:
show our love for others
in what we say and do.

Tell it together

Jesus said…

If you say you love me,
you must do what I told you to—
show your love for others
in what you say and do.

Echo:
**If we say we love you
we must do what you tell us to—
show our love for others
in what we say and do.**

I will talk to the Father
and I know that he will send
the Spirit of truth to help you
and be your constant friend.

You already know the Spirit
for you have eyes that see,
the Spirit will live in you
just as the Spirit lives in me.

If you say you love me,
you must do what I told you to—
show your love for others
in what you say and do.

Echo:
**If we say we love you
we must do what you tell us to—
show our love for others
in what we say and do.**

35

The gate
Jesus the good shepherd

For your reflection: John 10:1–18

In Jesus' time, people knew a lot about sheep. Often, a group of shepherds would gather their sheep together in a single enclosure or 'fold'. One of the shepherds would lie across the opening to protect the whole flock. The only way that thieves could get in was to sneak in over the wall. The relationship between sheep and shepherd was so close that the sheep would recognise their own shepherd's voice and follow him.

Jesus wanted people to understand what he himself was like, so he used what people already knew about shepherding to help them understand.

Tell-it tip

This is a simple reflection. There are three refrains in the story. Each one appears at the end of a verse and is said only once. Practise them together before you tell.

Try it together

You are my sheep. Come near, come near *(gesture to come)*.
You are my sheep. Take care, take care *(gesture safety)*.
You are my sheep. Oh hear, oh hear *(gesture to hear)*.

Tell it together

Come near, come near—you are like sheep in a pen.
See how the shepherd lies across the door? Wolves cannot get in.
Jesus said, 'I am the door to the sheep's fold;
rest safe and shelter from the cold.
I am the good shepherd. I keep watch and never sleep.
I give my life and lay it down for each and every sheep.
You are my sheep. Come near, come near *(gesture to come).*'

Take care, take care—there are thieves everywhere!
See how they sneak and creep over the wall to snatch the sheep?
    Beware!
They only want to destroy, harm your faith and maim.
Keep close to your shepherd. He knows each of you by name.
Jesus said, 'I am the good shepherd. I keep watch and never sleep.
I give my life and lay it down for each and every sheep.
You are my sheep. Take care, take care *(gesture safety).*'

Hear, oh hear—know your shepherd's voice.
See how his sheep walk with him and follow him by choice?
He leads them to green grassland, by water deep and still,
and guides them through each rocky place to a life that is rich
    and full.
Jesus said, 'I am the good shepherd. I keep watch and never sleep.
I give my life and lay it down for each and every sheep.
You are my sheep. Oh hear, oh hear *(gesture to hear).*'

36

Clippity cloppity
Jesus rides into Jerusalem

For your reflection: Matthew 21:1–11; Mark 11:1–11;
Luke 19:28–44

Jesus arrives in Jerusalem riding on a donkey, as foretold by the prophet Zechariah (Zechariah 9:9). Crowds gather to welcome him, cheering, waving palm branches and laying down their coats. They hail him as the king who will save them from their enemies and restore Israel. Some believe him to be a political figure, others the long-awaited Messiah and still others (who are not celebrating at all) as a threat. The latter tell Jesus to silence the adulation of the crowds.

Jesus' response not only affirms what is happening in front of them, but states that all of creation will recognise him and cry out in worship. This is even more poignant when considering the deity of Jesus and his role in the creation of the world.

Tell-it tips

This retelling has a tone of celebration, a strong pace and a gathering strength. It will require practice for a smooth and lyrical flow and should not be rushed. Participation can be done in one large group or divided between two groups. You may also want to ask both groups to speak their own parts together at the very end.

Phrases and actions for everyone to say and/or do together appear in bold below. You will want to try them together with your group before the story begins.

Try it together

Group 1

(Tap your knees in a walking rhythm)
Clippity cloppity clippity clop!
On, little donkey, and don't you stop.

Group 2

(Wave your hands in the air and sway)
The king is coming! The king is here!
Wave your palms and give a cheer!

Tell it together

Here comes Jesus! See him ride
On a donkey untamed, untried.

Group 1

(Tap your knees in a walking rhythm)
Clippity cloppity clippity clop!
On, little donkey, and don't you stop.

Group 2

(Wave your hands in the air and sway)
The king is coming! The king is here!
Wave your palms and give a cheer!

Through the streets of Jerusalem:
'Hosanna! to the Lord who comes!'

Group 1

(Tap your knees in a walking rhythm)
Clippity cloppity clippity clop!
On, little donkey, and don't you stop.

Group 2

(Wave your hands in the air and sway)
The king is coming! The king is here!
Wave your palms and give a cheer!

We spread our coats along the way.
The donkey doesn't buck or bray.

Group 1

(Tap your knees in a walking rhythm)
Clippity cloppity clippity clop!
On, little donkey, and don't you stop.

Group 2

(Wave your hands in the air and sway)
The king is coming! The king is here!
Wave your palms and give a cheer!

Someone said, 'Don't let them shout!
What's this nonsense all about?'
'I could stop them,' Jesus said.
'But the stones would still cry out!'

Group 1

(Tap your knees in a walking rhythm)
Clippity cloppity clippity clop!
On, little donkey, and don't you stop.

Group 2

(Wave your hands in the air and sway)
The king is coming! The king is here!
Wave your palms and give a cheer!

37

Please don't wash my feet
Jesus washes Peter's feet

For your reflection: John 13:1–17

Before eating his last supper with his disciples, Jesus washes their feet. Peter objects because it is a menial chore, undertaken by servants. However, Jesus is giving them an object lesson in the humility with which they are to treat others. He is also reminding them of the spiritual cleaning available to everyone. He tells Peter, 'If you don't let me wash you, you don't really belong to me.' Peter responds, 'Wash all of me!'

This retelling is from Peter's point of view. It captures both the tenderness and the toughness in his character and, ultimately, in our own as we seek to give more of ourselves to Jesus.

Tell-it tips

This story is, essentially, a participation poem. It is very tender in tone, simple and prayerful.

Try it together

These two refrains appear in the story. The first appears three times and the second appears once. Practise saying each one together.

Please don't wash my feet.

Please, Lord, wash my feet.

Tell it together

Please don't wash my feet.
I couldn't bear the shame;
the knowing that you know me
and would do it just the same.

Please don't wash my feet.
I couldn't bear the pain;
the knowing that I know you
holy—without blame.

Please don't wash my feet.
I should be washing you.
After everything I've heard you say
and all I've seen you do,

How could I let you wash my feet?
And yet, you say I must
if I am to love as you love
and walk each day in trust.

Please, Lord, wash my feet.
Wash my hands and head.
I am made of dust.
Wash all of me instead.

38

Communion

A prayer response to the Last Supper

For your reflection: Matthew 26:17–30; Mark 14:12–26; Luke 22:7–23

Plans are afoot to arrest and execute Jesus. He has been trying to prepare his disciples for this several times, although they have failed to understand. On the night of his arrest, he shares a last supper with them. It is rich with the symbolism that continues in Communion today. He breaks bread and likens it to his body, which will soon be broken. He pours the wine and likens it to the blood that will be spilt so that many can be forgiven. He tells them that whenever they eat like this in the future, they are to remember him.

The dark hours of the crucifixion lie just ahead. Jesus is arrested, betrayed by Judas and deserted by his disciples. How different their memory of this time together would have been if not for the resurrection.

Tell-it tips

This is a simple Communion prayer.

Try it together

Invite everyone to reflect on the words together.

Tell it together

I take this bread as if it were
a splinter from the cross,
where the raw flesh of God took on
my sin and what it cost.

I take this bread and eat it—
this body broken in pain—
I take this bread and remember
until you come again.

I take this wine as if it were
a drop of crimson blood,
washing through with cleansing power
from the Son of God.

I take this wine and drink it—
this blood that rids my stain—
I take this wine and remember
until you come again.

I take this cup as if it were
a symbol of your grave—
empty of all but hope,
proof of your power to save.

I take this cup and grasp it—
this promise I retain—
I take this cup and remember
that you will come again.

I take this life as if it were
mine and mine alone.
I take this life and give it back
as I bow before your throne.

I take this life and give it—
I long for you to reign—
I take your life and remember
that you will come again.

39

This is the garden
Judas betrays Jesus

For your reflection: Matthew 26:47–56; Mark 14:43–51;
Luke 22:47–53; John 18:1–11

During their last supper together, Jesus tells Peter that Peter will deny knowing him three times before the rooster crows. Despite his protests to the contrary, Peter does just that. And Peter is not the only one. Judas will betray Jesus to his enemies and the others too will doubt, despair or desert.

After supper, they all sing a hymn together and go into the garden. Jesus asks them to stay awake in prayer with him through that gruelling night in Gethsemane, but they all fall asleep.

This mini monologue retells the story of the arrest and could be the story of any one of several disciples, or indeed Mark, who is also thought to have been there.

Tell-it tips

There is a simple refrain with actions to do together before and after the story.

Try it together

Practise the refrain together.

This is the garden dark and still *(arms out)*
where Jesus prayed to do God's will *(hands together)*.

Tell it together

This is the garden dark and still *(arms out)*
where Jesus prayed to do God's will *(hands together)*.

It was dark and quiet in the garden. We had never seen Jesus so sad. He wanted us to pray with him, but our eyes were as heavy as our spirits.

It's hard to say which I heard first, the angry crowd or the voice of Jesus. 'Wake up!' he said.

I opened my eyes to the glow of torches; I saw clubs and swords and a familiar face. By the time I had jumped to my feet, Judas had walked up to Jesus and kissed him on the cheek as if they were friends.

'This is him,' Judas said to the soldiers with him.

'Judas,' I heard Jesus whisper. 'Are you betraying me like this?'

The next thing I knew, the crowd closed in. I was terrified! We all were. We didn't know what to do. Peter drew his sword and tried to defend Jesus. He even cut off the ear of the high priest's servant, Malchus.

'Put the sword down,' said Jesus. Then he touched Malchus' ear and healed him. 'Angels would come to my rescue if I asked them to! But I will do what must be done.'

All I could think to do was run.

This is the garden dark and still *(arms out)*
where Jesus prayed to do God's will *(hands together)*.

40

Jesus dies on a cross
The crucifixion

For your reflection: Matthew 27:1–51; Mark 15:1–37;
Luke 23:1–46; John 19:1–30

Jesus is nailed on to the cross and, astonishingly, prays, 'Father forgive them. They don't know what they're doing.' He has been beaten bloody and marched through the city carrying his own cross, dressed in a robe of scarlet. The robe has been torn from his back. He is wearing a crown of thorns. There is a sign on the cross which reads, 'This is Jesus, the King of the Jews.'

Some in the crowd insult him. One of the two criminals that are hanging beside Jesus ridicules him for being unable to save himself, let alone anyone else. The other shows faith in Jesus and is promised a place in the kingdom. Many of Jesus' loved ones are among the distraught witnesses. Jesus asks his close friend, John, to take care of his mother when he is gone.

At noon the sky turns black and stays that way until 3 pm. Then, at the moment of death, the land shakes and the temple curtain is torn in two. The Roman soldiers at the foot of the cross can't help but proclaim him to be the Son of God. His body is buried in a newly cut tomb that belongs to somebody else. All seems lost.

Tell-it tips

This is a simple reflective story. The participation comes after the story in the form of a simple blessing with actions. You will want to try it together before you start.

Try it together

God be with you *(form triangle with the pointer fingers and thumbs of both hands to symbolise the Trinity)*.

Jesus be with you *(arms straight out to the sides to symbolise the cross)*.

Spirit be with you *(hands out in front of you, palms up, to symbolise receiving the Spirit)*.

Tell it together

Jesus did not hate those who hated him.

He did not hate those who told lies about him.

He did not hate those who ordered him to die.

He did not hate those who beat him until he bled or pushed a thorny crown on to his head.

He did not hate the soldiers who led him to be killed.

He did not hate them when they nailed him to a cross.

He did not hate those who stood jeering on the hill.

'If you are the one God sent, come down from the cross. You can't even save yourself. How can you save us?'

Jesus did not hate his enemies.

He loved them instead. 'Father, forgive them,' he said.

Many who loved Jesus were also there, watching and weeping and waiting.

It took long hours for Jesus to die.

The sky went dark.

'My God, my God,' Jesus cried, 'why have you left me all alone?'

When the time had come, Jesus whispered, 'It is done!'

Then Jesus died for everyone.

God be with you *(form triangle with fingers and thumbs)*.
Jesus be with you *(arms straight out to the sides)*.
Spirit be with you *(hands out in front of you, palms up)*.

41

come early to the tomb
Jesus is risen

For your reflection: John 20:1–18

Early on Sunday morning, when the sabbath is over, several of Jesus' women followers go to the tomb to finish preparing his body for burial. By this time, an angel has already rolled the stone away and Jesus is gone. This retelling focuses on the resurrection account found in the Gospel of John. It captures the excitement and emotion of the resurrection, its immense implications for the whole world and the personal and tender impact on each of us when Jesus so tenderly calls our name.

Tell-it tips

This story is full of passion and pathos, powerful and engaging. You will want to prepare it very well before you tell. Pay particular attention to how you will use your voice and facial expressions (see pages 19–21).

Try it together

Encourage the group to engage their imaginations fully as they listen. Set the scene: Jesus has been dead for three days and everyone is distraught. Ask solid reflective questions afterwards: Who were they imagining themselves to be in the story? How did they feel?

Tell it together

Come early to the tomb with Mary,
before the light of day.
Come with all of your sorrow
and see the stone is rolled away!

Run and tell Peter and John!
Run all the way from the tomb.
'They've taken his body from where it lay
And left an empty room!'

Run as fast as you can with Peter.
Run faster yet with John.
Peek in and see the linen strips—
but where has Jesus' body gone?

Step into the tomb with Peter.
Look around everywhere.
The cloth which had been on Jesus' head
is folded up on its own with care.

John is now beside Peter,
understanding what Jesus had said;
believing now, with his own eyes,
that Jesus would rise from the dead.

Will you go home now with Peter and John,
or stay with Mary outside the tomb?
See how she weeps and stoops again,
looking into the empty room.

Can you see two angels sitting
where Jesus' head and feet used to be?
They are dressed in white and saying,
'Mary, why do you weep?'

She is speaking through her sobs:
'Someone has taken my Lord away!
I don't know where they've taken him
or where his body lay!'

Turn around with Mary.
See who is standing there.
She thinks it is the gardener,
but it is Jesus coming near.

'Why are you crying?' he asks.
'Who are you looking for?'
'Oh sir,' she cries, 'have you taken him?
Where can I find my Lord?'

Come early to the tomb with Mary.
Hear Jesus whisper her name.
Hear her reply, 'Oh Rabbi!'
in a whisper just the same.

Come early to the tomb with Mary
before the light of day.
Come with all of your sorrow
and see the stone is rolled away!

42

On the road to Emmaus

Jesus walks with friends on the road

For your reflection: Luke 24:13–35

On the day of his resurrection, Jesus joins two despairing travellers on their seven-mile journey between Jerusalem and Emmaus. They do not recognise him. They tell him they have heard a rumour that Jesus is alive but don't believe it. They describe the crucifixion, the loss of Jesus and their dashed hopes in him as the Messiah. Jesus does not reveal his identity but reminds them of all of the prophecies that point to the Messiah's suffering and resurrection. It is only later, as Jesus breaks bread, that they recognise who they have been travelling with. They run back to Jerusalem to tell the disciples that Jesus is not dead!

The retelling is a travel tale and captures the despair and joy of the journey.

Tell-it tips

This story has a strong rhythmic pace to represent the feeling of journey.

Try it together

Everyone repeats the following refrain together throughout. Practise with a gesture so that everyone in the group will know when to join in.

We walked on the road to Emmaus.
We talked on the road to Emmaus.

Tell it together

Three days after Jesus died
we walked on the road to Emmaus,
we talked on the road to Emmaus,
we cried on the road to Emmaus.

Three days after Jesus died
we felt lost on the road to Emmaus.

Three days after Jesus died
we met a man on the road to Emmaus.
We walked on the road to Emmaus.
We talked on the road to Emmaus.

'Who was this Jesus who died?' he asked.
We told all on the road to Emmaus.

How he was born and lived and died,
and on a cross was crucified,
and in a tomb behind a stone
was buried there.

How some women went to tend with care
the body they thought buried there
and found the stone was rolled away,
and the body gone from where it lay
and angels singing, 'He is risen!'

Jesus is alive again, they say, but how?
And how can a dead man save us now?

'Oh foolish friends,' the stranger said.
Three days ago your Saviour died,
just as the prophets prophesied.

Why do you now doubt this story?
Jesus said he would suffer,
then enter glory!
Remember what the scriptures tell us?'

We walked on the road to Emmaus.
We talked on the road to Emmaus.
He told all on the road to Emmaus.

We got to Emmaus at evening time
and invited the stranger to stay and dine.

He sat with us in Emmaus.
He blessed our bread in Emmaus.
He broke it too, as Jesus had,
and shared it.

It was then we began to recognise
something familiar in his eyes.
Could it be true?
Three days after Jesus died,
he shared our bread in Emmaus!

And just as we knew who he was,
he was gone.

We hurried back to tell the others.
'Jesus is alive!
We have seen him too!' we said.
'We just didn't know him
until we shared the broken bread.'

New Testament parables

43

Kingdom round
Parables of God's kingdom

For your reflection: Matthew 13; Mark 4; Luke 13

Jesus uses several short parables to reveal mysteries about God's kingdom and help us to understand what God's king is like. The parables of the yeast and the mustard seed speak of the emergence and growth of God's kingdom in the world. The hidden treasure and the pearl speak of the decisions we make when becoming part of God's kingdom. The parable of the dragnet speaks of the consequences of rejecting God's kingdom, while the growing seed speaks of themes of quiet growth and harvest. This story is a cluster of some of Jesus' kingdom teachings.

Tell-it tips

Each verse represents one parable, and is spoken. The refrain can, of course, be spoken. However, it can also be sung as a two- or four-part round, to the tune of 'Make new friends'. You can find the tune in *The Round Book* by Margaret Read MacDonald and Winifred Jaegar or via an online search.

You may choose to tell all the verses or pick and choose which verses you want to include. It also works well if you tell it as a series—one verse per session and then all the verses when the series is complete.

Try it together

Practise the following refrain together.

**Spread God's love; a little love will bring
the kingdom of heaven into everything.**

Tell it together

God's kingdom is like the yeast that grows
and spreads throughout the whole of the dough.
It quietly works to make the bread rise
higher and higher before our eyes.

**Spread God's love; a little love will bring
the kingdom of heaven into everything.**

God's kingdom is like the seed so small
that becomes the biggest tree of all,
branches reaching to the sky,
birds resting way up high.

**Spread God's love; a little love will bring
the kingdom of heaven into everything.**

God's kingdom is like a treasure that's found
buried deeply under the ground.
The one who finds it knows what it will yield
and sells everything to buy the whole field.

**Spread God's love; a little love will bring
the kingdom of heaven into everything.**

The kingdom is like the one who buys
the rarest of pearls that he looks for and spies,
and sells what he owns to own this one thing,
the most precious jewel and none of the bling.

**Spread God's love; a little love will bring
the kingdom of heaven into everything.**

God's kingdom is like scattered seed
that grows mysteriously while we sleep,
and all in good time it is time to bring
heaven near and the harvest in.

**Spread God's love; a little love will bring
the kingdom of heaven into everything.**

God's kingdom is like a fishing net
full of fish; but let's not forget,
some are not ready, will be thrown away.
Hear what Jesus has to say.

**Spread God's love; a little love will bring
the kingdom of heaven into everything.**

The more you give yourself to God,
the more you know it's true:
God's kingdom is not just in heaven,
God's kingdom is in you.

44

Tom Farmer
The kingdom quietly grows

For your reflection: Mark 4:26–29

In this parable, Jesus reminds us that the growth of God's kingdom is an everyday mystery. Once the seeds are scattered, they grow in unknown ways, continuously and quietly while the farmer gets on with the other things he has to do. Though the seed is unseen to begin with, it grows into a huge harvest. This deceptively simple parable engages us in a variety of ways. The retelling captures the process, including the patience, faith and trust inherent in waiting for God's kingdom to grow.

Tell-it tips

This story can be sung to the traditional tune of 'Oats, peas, beans and barley grow' and is ideal for harvest celebrations. It can also be told without music. The refrain is sung or said together between each verse. You will want to try it together a few times before telling.

Also, invite people to join you in the actions during the verses as you go along. They appear in bold italics below.

Try it together

Practise this refrain together as you pretend to be a small seed, growing tall.

Oats, peas, beans and barley grow,
Oats, peas, beans and barley grow.
I wonder, do you wonder how
oats, peas, beans and barley grow?

Tell it together

(Pretend to be a small seed growing tall)

Oats, peas, beans and barley grow,
Oats, peas, beans and barley grow.
I wonder, do you wonder how
oats, peas, beans and barley grow?

First Tom Farmer plants the seed *(scatter seeds)*,
then he rests and takes his ease *(head on hands)*,
and while he's sleeping peacefully *(whisper with finger to mouth in a hush)*
oats, peas, beans and barley grow.

Oats, peas, beans and barley grow,
Oats, peas, beans and barley grow.
I wonder, do you wonder how
oats, peas, beans and barley grow?

Cockerel crows to sing the dawn *(cock-a-doodle-doo)*.
Wake up, Tom, it's early morn *(rub eyes)*.
Cows need milking in the barn *(moo)*
while oats, peas, beans and barley grow.

Oats, peas, beans and barley grow,
Oats, peas, beans and barley grow.
I wonder, do you wonder how
oats, peas, beans and barley grow?

The horse needs feed, the pigs need corn *(pretend to tip a bucket)*,
the goat needs oats, lambs need born *(baaaaaa)*.
Fence needs fixed, the hay needs mown *(pretend to hammer nail)*
while oats, peas, beans and barley grow.

Oats, peas, beans and barley grow,
Oats, peas, beans and barley grow.
I wonder, do you wonder how
oats, peas, beans and barley grow?

Waiting for the harvest sing *(link arms with people on either side)*,
waiting for the harvesting *(link arms in the opposite direction)*.
Hey, Tom, is it time to bring
the oats, peas, beans and barley in?

Oats, peas, beans and barley grow,
Oats, peas, beans and barley grow.
I wonder, do you wonder how
oats, peas, beans and barley grow?

You and I can root and grow *(point to the person next to you and
then yourself)*.
You and I can root and grow *(point out to another person near you
and then yourself)*.
I wonder, do you wonder how *(shrug shoulders quizzically)*
you and I can root and grow?

Oats, peas, beans and barley grow,
Oats, peas, beans and barley grow.
I wonder, do you wonder how
oats, peas, beans and barley grow?

Waiting on the Lord today *(pretend to pray)*,
believe what Jesus has to say *(open a Bible)*.
God's Spirit helps us root and grow,
trusting in the Lord each day.

Oats, peas, beans and barley grow,
Oats, peas, beans and barley grow.
I wonder, do you wonder how
oats, peas, beans and barley grow?

45

Farmer Friendly's simple deed

The sower and four soils

For your reflection: Matthew 13:3–9, 18–23; Mark 4:3–9, 13–20; Luke 8:5–8, 11–15

Jesus knows that not everyone will accept his teachings. He tells a story about a sower who scatters seeds (representing those who spread his teachings). Some seeds fall on the road and are eaten by birds (snatched away by Satan). Some land on shallow, stony ground and spring up quickly but dies (don't develop spiritual roots so can't grow properly). Some are choked out by thorns (other interests and priorities). However, some land on good soil and produce a great harvest. These are people who accept what Jesus has to say for themselves and pass it on to others.

Tell-it tips

This story is a retelling of Jesus' parable of the sower. Invite your group to join you in the actions as you tell the story.

Try it together

Invite your group to do the actions in the story with you as you go along.

Tell it together

'Twas Farmer Friendly's simple deed *(point to yourself with your right thumb)*
to scatter round her lots of seed *(pretend to scatter seed with your right hand)*.
Some fell where it could not grow *(lay the palm of your left hand flat out in front of you, sharply)*,
got eaten by a big black crow *(form your right hand into a 'beak'; swoop it down and pretend to eat seeds from your left palm)*.

Some sprang high in a rocky place *(show backs of hands and wiggle fingers up in the air like plants)*,
was withered by the sun's bright face *(bring hands and fingers down as if plants are wilting)*.
Some fell among a crowd of weeds *(put palms together; fingers pointing upwards and intertwined; wriggle fingers like plants)*
that crushed and choked the growing seeds *(fold fingers down and bring hands down as if plants have been choked)*.

I wonder, do you wonder *(pointer finger of right hand on chin as if asking a question)*:
how will Farmer Friendly sow
to help the seeds take root and grow *(hold hands out quizzically)*?

She ploughs her field *(pretend to dig)*,
pulls out the weeds *(pretend to pull stubborn weeds)*,
picks the rocks *(pretend to lift heavy rocks)*
and plants the seeds *(pretend to plant seeds carefully)*.

In good soil the roots take hold *(wiggle fingers of both hands downwards to signify roots)*,
the crops increase by hundredfold *(wiggle fingers upward and raise arms in the air, with backs of hands facing out)*.

I wonder, do you wonder *(pointer finger of right hand on chin as if asking a question)*:
how will we sow
to help God's love take root and grow *(hands on heart)*?

We'll pray a bit *(fold hands in prayer)*,
we'll talk a bit *(move hands as if talking to each other)*,
we'll make a friend today *(clasp hands together as if in friendship)*.
Bit by bit God's crop will grow *(forefinger and thumb of each hand widening bit by bit)*.
Away, you crows, away! *(hands sweeping up and out as if shooing crows away)*

46

Up the hill
The good Samaritan

For your reflection: Luke 10:30–37

One day, Jesus tells a Jewish teacher that the two most important laws are to love God and to love your neighbour. The teacher asks Jesus, 'Who is my neighbour?' The story of the Samaritan comes as his reply.

In it, a man walking the deserted road from Jerusalem to Jericho is attacked and left for dead. A priest and a temple worker, who might have been expected to help, walk by. A Samaritan (one of a group that are ill-regarded by Jews) goes above and beyond to help. Jesus then asks his Jewish questioner which of the three was a good neighbour. The teacher says, 'The one who showed compassion.' Jesus says, 'Go and do the same.'

Tell-it tips

This is a finger story and borrows its gestures from the ever-popular nursery story 'Mr Wiggle and Mr Waggle'. It is simple and fun. You will want to try the 'refrain' together before you begin. It is repeated throughout the story with different voices and at different speeds.

Note: Toward the end of the story and for two verses only, the refrain changes to 'Giddy up the hill'. This is because the Samaritan is on a donkey. Let this be a surprise as you get to it. Your audience will appreciate the humour and join in without preparation.

Try it together

Practise the refrain together.

Up the hill *(thumb up, moving in an upward direction)*
and down the hill *(thumb down, moving in a downward direction)*,
up the hill *(thumb up, moving in an upward direction)*
and down the hill *(thumb down, moving in a downward direction)*.

Tell it together

There was once a road, a lonely road, a dangerous road…

Up the hill *(thumb up, moving in an upward direction)*
and down the hill *(thumb down, moving in a downward direction)*,
up the hill *(thumb up, moving in an upward direction)*
and down the hill *(thumb down, moving in a downward direction)*.

It was also the only road—which is why a man went walking…

Up the hill *(thumb up, moving in an upward direction)*
and down the hill *(thumb down, moving in a downward direction)*,
up the hill *(thumb up, moving in an upward direction)*
and down the hill *(thumb down, moving in a downward direction)*.

Suddenly, robbers jumped out! They hit him on the head and took everything he had. They left him lying half dead and quickly ran away…

Repeat quickly:

Up the hill *(thumb up, moving in an upward direction)*
and down the hill *(thumb down, moving in a downward direction)*,

up the hill *(thumb up, moving in an upward direction)*
and down the hill *(thumb down, moving in a downward direction).*

All seemed hopeless for the injured man until a priest came by…

Repeat in a holier-than-thou fashion:

Up the hill *(thumb up, moving in an upward direction)*
and down the hill *(thumb down, moving in a downward direction),*
up the hill *(thumb up, moving in an upward direction)*
and down the hill *(thumb down, moving in a downward direction).*

He saw the man but crossed to the other side and kept on going…

Repeat in a holier-than-thou fashion:

Up the hill *(thumb up, moving in an upward direction)*
and down the hill *(thumb down, moving in a downward direction),*
up the hill *(thumb up, moving in an upward direction)*
and down the hill *(thumb down, moving in a downward direction).*

After a while, a person who helped in the temple came by…

Repeat in a flustered manner:

Up the hill *(thumb up, moving in an upward direction)*
and down the hill *(thumb down, moving in a downward direction),*
up the hill *(thumb up, moving in an upward direction)*
and down the hill *(thumb down, moving in a downward direction).*

He saw the man too. He even walked up and looked at him. But, in the end, he too kept on going…

Repeat in a flustered manner:

Up the hill *(thumb up, moving in an upward direction)*
and down the hill *(thumb down, moving in a downward direction)*,
up the hill *(thumb up, moving in an upward direction)*
and down the hill *(thumb down, moving in a downward direction)*.

Finally, the man's enemy came along on his donkey…

Repeat as if swaying on the back of a donkey:

Giddy up the hill *(thumb up, moving in an upward direction)*
and down the hill *(thumb down, moving in a downward direction)*,
giddy up the hill *(thumb up, moving in an upward direction)*
and down the hill *(thumb down, moving in a downward direction)*.

When he saw the man, he felt compassion for him and decided to help. He soothed the man and bandaged his wounds as best he could. Then he put the man on his own donkey and took him…

Repeat as if swaying on the back of a donkey:

Giddy up the hill *(thumb up, moving in an upward direction)*
and down the hill *(thumb down, moving in a downward direction)*,
giddy up the hill *(thumb up, moving in an upward direction)*
and down the hill *(thumb down, moving in a downward direction)*.

He found a place for the man to stay and recover. He even paid for the man's bills and promised to pay even more if needed.

Now Jesus asked a question, 'Who was the good neighbour in this story and what did he do? You must go and be a good neighbour too…'

Up the hill *(thumb up, moving in an upward direction)*
and down the hill *(thumb down, moving in a downward direction)*,
up the hill *(thumb up, moving in an upward direction)*
and down the hill *(thumb down, moving in a downward direction)*.

47

Tired Tim's sleepless night
The friend at midnight

For your reflection: Luke 11:5–13

Jesus often tells parables—short stories that we can easily imagine—to help us in our spiritual understanding. The parable of the friend at midnight teaches us about the need for persistent prayer. In it, a friend eventually agrees to help his neighbour due to the neighbour's persistence, despite the late hour and inconvenience of being woken up for bread when everyone is asleep. Through it, we are reminded to pray without giving up for anything needed by ourselves and others.

Tell-it tips

This retelling has been written as a light-hearted nursery rhyme and involves everyone in a simple refrain and other actions.

Try it together

Practise the following refrain together.

Tap tappit! Tap tappit! *(mime knocking on your hand)*

Practise the actions in response to the phrases 'peeking out' and 'peeking in'.

- Peeking out *(mime peeking with right hand over eyes)*
- Peeking in *(mime peeking with left hand over eyes)*

Tell it together

Now who is this tapping
on Tired Tim's door?
Tap tappit! Tap tappit! *(mime knocking on your hand)*
At midnight or more?

Tired Tim's peeking out *(right hand over eyes)*.
Pesky Pete's peeking in *(left hand over eyes)*.
'Have you got any bread?'
he says with a grin.

'Pete, you're a pest.
Please come back when it's day!'
I wonder, do you wonder:
will Pete go away?

Now who is this tapping
on Tired Tim's door?
Tap tappit! Tap tappit! *(mime knocking on your hand)*
interrupting a snore!

Tired Tim's peeking out *(right hand over eyes)*.
Pesky Pete's peeking in *(left hand over eyes)*.
'The bread is for a friend,'
he says. 'Please let me in'.

'Please, Pesky Pete,
come back when it's day!'
I wonder, do you wonder:
will Pete go away?

Now who is this tapping
on Tired Tim's door?
Tap tappit! Tap tappit! *(mime knocking on your hand)*
We've heard it before!

Tired Tim's peeking out *(right hand over eyes)*.
Pesky Pete's peeking in *(left hand over eyes)*.
'All right,' says Tim,
There's some bread in my bin!'

I wonder, do you wonder:
does God have a clock?
When we pray, night or day,
God is there when we knock.

48

The honest man's prayer

The Pharisee and the tax collector

For your reflection: Luke 18:9–14

Jesus tells the parable of the Pharisee and the tax collector in response to those who are confident in their own righteousness and look down on everyone else. In it, the attitude and consequent prayers of two men are compared. Jesus praises the attitude and prayer of the man most looked down upon. Jesus says, 'Those who exalt themselves will be humbled, but those who are humble will be exalted.'

Tell-it tips

This story has an element of tableau in it. You will be like a sculptor creating a posed scene with two volunteers from your group. One will be a pious Pharisee and the other a humble tax collector.

The story also has an action refrain for everyone to do together.

Try it together

Practise the refrain a few times together, then ask everyone to sit down, ready for the story. Let them know that their part will take place at the very end of the story and you will let them know when you get there.

If you pray for show, God will know *(pose like a proud Pharisee: stand tall and stiff, nose in the air, hands raised, pious face, one eye open).*

If you pray from your heart, God will hear *(pose standing, head bowed, eyes closed, hands folded).*

For the tableau, choose two volunteers and create a posed scene as below.

* Silently shape the first volunteer into the proud and pious Pharisee (standing tall and stiff, nose in the air, hands raised, pious face, one eye open).
* Silently shape the second volunteer into the humble and sincere tax collector (standing, head bowed, eyes closed, hands folded).

Stand between the two to start your story and follow the direction as you go along.

Tell it together

Jesus told this story to some people who thought they were better than others.

Two men went to the temple to pray *(acknowledge each with a gesture and a nod).*

One man thought he was better than the other *(point to the Pharisee and stand beside him).* The Pharisee stood up proud and prayed out loud.

'Thank you, God. I am so good. I always do the things I should. I give my money. I keep the rules. I spend my time in prayer. I'm not like that man over there.' *(Turn the Pharisee's head in the direction of the tax collector; point a thumb or hand in the direction of the tax collector.)*

The tax collector knew he wasn't always good *(gesture to the tax collector and stand beside him)*. He didn't always do the things he should. He hung his head and sadly said:

'Forgive me, God, for the things I've done. I know that I'm the guilty one.' *(Move to the middle again)*

Which prayer do you think God answered? Jesus said *(signal everyone to stand and say the refrain)*:

If you pray for show, God will know *(stand tall and stiff, nose in the air, hands raised, pious face, one eye open)*.
If you pray from your heart, God will hear *(pose standing, head bowed, eyes closed, hands folded)*.

Ask everyone to sit. Silently unfreeze each character in the tableau back to themselves and send them back to their seats.

49

A change of heart
Two sons

For your reflection: Matthew 21:28–32

In this parable of two sons, Jesus speaks to the hypocrisy of those who say they are committed to God but really aren't. Actions speak louder than words.

Tell-it tips

This story works well in a number of ways. You could simply tell the story yourself and invite your group to do the gestures with you as you come to them, or you could choose three people to tell the story together. You could also choose three people to mime the action as you go along. I have written it here as a group tale and mime.

Try it together

You will want to choose three tellers who are confident readers and speakers, and three people to mime the action. For a smoother, more polished feel, gather and rehearse before your large group arrives. For a more ad-lib and improvised feel, choose volunteers on the spot.

It is important that your tellers feel confident in their reading and speaking skills. In either case, keep in mind that you are aiming for the feeling of a well-told story rather than a dramatic performance.

Guidance for possible actions is written into the text below.

Tell it together

Teller 1:	A man had a vineyard and lots of work to do.
Dad:	*(Mime 'big' and nod)*
Teller 2:	He also had two sons, and thought…
Dad:	*(Thinking face; tap chin; click fingers)*
Teller 3:	'I'll ask for their help too!'
Dad:	*(Determined nod)*
Teller 1:	'Will you come and help me?'
Dad:	*(Turn to older son and mime asking)*
Teller 2:	he asked his oldest son.
Dad:	*(Thumbs up hopefully)*
Teller 3:	'The harvest is ready and there's lots of work to be done.'
Dad:	*(Mime 'big' and nod)*
Teller 1:	'Find someone else to do it, Dad,'
Older son:	*(Shake head)*
Teller 2:	the son was quick to say.
Older Son:	*(Thumb down)*
Teller 3:	But just as quick, he was sorry
Older son:	*(Sorry face; thumbs up)*
Teller 1:	and went out and worked all day.
Older son:	*(Smile and pretend to dig)*
Teller 2:	When the youngest son was asked to help,
Dad:	*(Turn to younger son and mime asking)*
Teller 3:	he said, 'Sure, Dad! I'll be right there!'
Younger son:	*(Nod yes; thumbs up)*
Teller 1:	But no one saw him all day long. He never did appear.
Dad:	*(Mime searching)*

Teller 2:	Jesus asked those who were listening,
Dad:	*(Hands to ears)*
Teller 3:	'Which son obeyed his father best?'
Dad:	*(Shrug shoulders quizzically)*
Teller 1:	The son who said he wouldn't help but did
Dad:	*(Turn to the older son)*
Teller 2:	or the one who didn't mean his 'yes?'
Dad:	*(Turn to the youngest son)*
Teller 3:	Jesus told this story so that we would know it's true:
All:	what we do is more important than what we say we'll do.
Dad:	*(Nod)*

50

The good shepherd

The lost sheep

For your reflection: Matthew 18:12–14; Luke 15:3–7;
John 10:11–15

Jesus tells three parables after the Pharisees and religious leaders have accused him of welcoming and eating with 'sinners'. The key theme of all three (the lost coin, lost sheep and lost son) is redemption—how God loves, looks for and welcomes those who are far from him and excluded by others.

In the parable of the lost sheep, one sheep has gone missing from a flock of 100. The shepherd searches for it, finds it and brings it home.

Tell-it tips

This is a simple response story in which actions are done in response to the words shown in block capitals. Try it together before you begin.

Try it together

Practise the actions before you start.

- SHEPHERD *(make a hook by putting your arm up in the air and crooking your hand)*
- SHEEP *(baaa)*
- LEAP *(leap, if you have room, or stand up and sit down quickly)*

Tell it together

If a SHEPHERD has a lot of SHEEP and one SHEEP LEAPS away,
he leaves the lot safe on the spot for the SHEEP that LEAPS away.
The SHEPHERD will look everywhere. He will walk and climb
   and run.
Day or night he will never stop until he finds that one.
He brings the SHEEP home safe and sound
and LEAPS for joy that his SHEEP is found.

Heaven has a happy day
when anyone chooses to live God's way.
'I am the good SHEPHERD,' Jesus said. 'I know all my SHEEP
   by name.
No matter where they wander, I love them just the same.
I will give my life to save them, no matter what the cost.
If you want to follow me, you too must love those who are lost.'

Further resources

I am often asked to recommend storytelling resources. At the top of this list are those produced by Bob Hartman, who has also played a huge role in promoting storytelling and encouraging storytellers. *Anyone Can Tell a Bible Story*, *Telling the Bible* and *Telling the Gospel* (Monarch, 2011, 2015) are must-haves for those interested in prop-free, performance-flavoured storytelling.

Martyn Payne is masterful at telling stories in a variety of different ways. *Creative Ways to Tell a Bible Story* (BRF, 2013) is an invaluable resource and totally lives up to its name. (See overleaf for more information.)

Among the many brilliant storytelling resources by Steven James is the *Creative Storytelling Guide for Children's Ministry* (Standard, 2003), which includes self-directed workshop materials to use with your own young people.

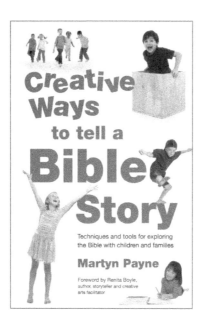

This resource offers a treasure trove of ideas for opening up a Bible story (the way in), telling the story (the way through) and exploring the meaning of the story (the way out), including suggestions for reflecting on how to apply the story to our lives today. These ideas will lift any Bible story off the page and into the hearts and minds of children and adults.

Creative Ways to Tell a Bible Story
Techniques and tools for exploring the Bible with children and families
Martyn Payne
ISBN 978 0 85746 113 1 £8.99

brfonline.org.uk

BRF

Transforming
lives and communities

Christian growth and understanding of the Bible

Resourcing individuals, groups and leaders in churches for their own spiritual journey and for their ministry

Church outreach in the local community

Offering three programmes that churches are embracing to great effect as they seek to engage with their local communities and transform lives

Teaching Christianity in primary schools

Working with children and teachers to explore Christianity creatively and confidently

Children's and family ministry

Working with churches and families to explore Christianity creatively and bring the Bible alive